Technology
In the
Classroom

VOLUME 1

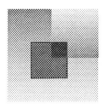

Technology in the Classroom

Volume 1

EDITED BY GARY FROELICH

COMAP, Inc.

Lexington, Massachussetts

A project of Consortium for Mathematics and Its Applications
Lexington, MA
ISBN 0–912843–32–2

Copyright © 1994 by COMAP, Inc. All rights reserved.
Suite 210
57 Bedford Street
Lexington, MA 02173
1–800–77–COMAP

Printed in the United States of America.

Contents

Acknowledgements

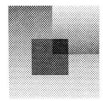

COMAP would like to acknowledge the National Science Foundation, whose support of the High School Mathematics and Its Applications Project made *Consortium* possible. In addition, we are grateful to Irwin Hoffman and Benjamin Levy, co-editors of the Computers column, for their contributions to *Consortium* and to this book; and to Roger Slade, Creative Director; Philip McGaw, Production Manager; Laurie Holbrook, Senior Copy Editor; Emily Sacca, Copy Editor; and Julie Olsen, Design Intern, for their production of this book.

Introduction

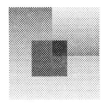

BENJAMIN N. LEVY

I t's an exciting time to teach mathematics! Technology, in the form of computers and graphing calculators, is prompting a fundamental rethinking of school mathematics. The National Council of Teachers of Mathematics published its *Curriculum and Evaluation Standards for School Mathematics* just as technology was becoming prominent. Yet the authors of the *Standards* did recognize that "new technology not only has made calculations and graphing easier, it has changed the very nature of the problems important to mathematics and the methods mathematicians use to investigate them."

This welcome collection from the pages of *Consortium* shows how creative teachers in different schools around the nation use technology to enhance mathematics for their students. In several of these articles, a student has joined a teacher to report an interesting classroom application. It is particularly heartening that these innovative and energetic individuals do have the advantage of technology in their classrooms.

In a way, these articles give a brief survey of the history of technology in the mathematics curriculum. Only a few years ago, programming on a remote computer was the primary means of innovation. Exercises in BASIC and, more recently, Pascal, gave interested students an opportunity to create useful and exciting applications. Now, happily, teachers have powerful and versatile software tools to engage the full range of students.

Geometry courses have been revitalized, some would even say "rescued," by pioneering software like the *Geometric Supposer*. Algebra has been less significantly affected by software, but the introduction and widespread use of hand-held graphing devices is beginning to have an effect. We look forward to greater use of symbolic manipulators like the *Mathematics Exploration Toolkit* and its successors.

As you read this collection, think ahead to emerging interactive and multimedia technologies. The pedagogy to approach significant new mathematical problems and to investigate them by new methods is outlined in these pages. The authors invite you to continue supporting the extension of the benefits of technology in classrooms everywhere. ❑

Benjamin N. Levy, Co-Editor of Computers Department, Consortium, is a teacher and consultant on mathematics education and technology. In 1989, he received an Edythe May Sliffe Award for Distinguished High School Teaching from the Mathematical Association of America.

Section 1

The articles in this section include programs and routines written in either Pascal or BASIC. There are also two articles that discuss the use of unusual pieces of hardware. Some are contributions of people who were high school students at the time the article was written. In reading these articles, one wonders what these remarkable students have accomplished since, and in what way the publication of their ideas while they were still in high school has affected their lives.

SPRING 1987

JOHN MCLAUGHLIN

The Lesson That Mushroomed

A Tale of Student Initiative

Editor's Note: It is not suggested that programs in Pascal use standard identifiers, such as input and output, as names of programmer-defined procedures. The use of FORWARD declaration in the program allowed for the interesting example of mutual recursion demonstrated in the program. It served to define a procedure before it was used, a necessary requirement in Pascal.

The flexibility shown by the author of this article in changing the curriculum to take advantage of student interest is the tool of a competent teacher. The advocates of strict lesson plans and those administrators enforcing such authoritative "fiat" are stripping the creativity from instruction and, as a consequence, prolonging the ennui in our classrooms.
—Irwin Hoffman, Ed.

A lesson designed to introduce computer math students to some basic theory of computer technology—the utilization of zeros and ones to represent the flow of information—recently mushroomed into a surprisingly effective unit covering several features of the Pascal programming language. The preliminary discussion of place values and arithmetic calculations in base two led to arithmetic operations in other bases. Class interest was stimulated and a student wrote a Pascal program to convert base-ten integers into equivalent base-two numbers. The natural extension of this idea was to write a more sophisticated program that converted numbers in bases less than ten to base-ten values.

The students extended these ideas into the study of hexadecimal numbers. They wanted to write the more demanding programs. The class is currently working in small groups to write a program that will add, subtract, and multiply base-16 numbers, printing the results in hexadecimal notation. These answers will then be converted into base-ten numbers for verification purposes.

The development of the programs included in this "grassroots" unit presented very convenient ways to introduce the ASCII code as well as such features of the Pascal language as the ORD and CHR functions and the CHAR, STRING, and LONG-INTEGER variables. Useful applications developed for the EOLN character and the FORWARD declaration statement.

The program included in this article was written by a Thomas Jefferson senior, Mark Havens, a student with one year of Pascal background. The assignment was to write a program to permit user input of a hexadecimal numeral and output of the base-ten equivalent value. Although not included in the article, Mark also wrote a program to permit input of any base between two and 36. He assumed the usage of the alphabet beyond the letter *F* to provide the necessary symbols. ❑

(Program written in UCSD Pascal on an Apple 2E.)

```
PROGRAM BASES__TO__10;
    (*CHANGES A NUMBER IN ANY BASE UNDER 37*)
VAR N: STRINGS; (*TO A BASE 10 NUMBER*)
J, SUB, B,K,C,S: INTEGER;
X: ARRAY [1..10] OF CHAR;
PROCEDURE OVER: FORWARD:
    (*ALERTS COMPUTER THAT THIS WILL BE USED
    LATER*)
PROCEDURE INPUT; (*INPUT NUMBER*)
BEGIN
WRITE ('TYPE IN BASE LESS THAN 17:');
READLN (C);
J: = 0;
SUB: = 1:
WRITE ('TYPE IN A NUMBER IN THAT BASE:');
WHILE NOT EOLN DO
BEGIN
READ (X[SUB]);
IF (ORD(X[SUB]) –55) > = C THEN
    (*STARTS OVER IF CHARACTER ISN'T IN *)

BEGIN (*THE GIVEN BASE*)
WRITE ('THIS IS NOT A BASE',C,' NUMBER');
WRITELN;
OVER;
END;
SUB: = SUB + 1;
J: = SUB;
END;
END;

PROCEDURE ACCUMULATE;
    (*CHANGES NUMBER INTO BASE 10*)
BEGIN
S: = 0;
B: = 1;
FOR K: = SUB – 2 DOWNTO 1 DO
BEGIN
IF X[K] < = CHR(57) THEN
    S: = S + (ORD (X[K]) – 48)*B;
IF X[K] > CHR(57) THEN
    S: = S + (ORD (X[K]) – 55)*B;
```

```
B: = B*C;
END;
END;

PROCEDURE OUTPUT; (*PRINTS NUMBER*)
BEGIN
FOR K: = 1 TO J – 2 DO
WRITE (X[K]);
WRITELN ('BASE ',C,' = ',S,' BASE10');
END;
PROCEDURE OVER; (*USED IN PROCEDURE
    INPUT TO START OVER*)
BEGIN
INPUT;
ACCUMULATE;
OUTPUT; EXIT (PROGRAM)
END;

BEGIN(*MAIN PROGRAM*)
INPUT;
ACCUMULATE;
OUTPUT;
END.
```

```
Output
3759 base 10 = 3759 base 10
11011011 base 2 = 219 base 10
11100011 base 2 = 227 base 10
FF base 16 = 3562 base 10
DEA base 16 = 3562 base 10
JGH base 20 = 7937 base 10
```

Summer 1988

JOHN WATERMAN
STUART OBERMAN
BRIAN MCQUIDDY

Bit by Byte:

A Study in Fractal Growth

Editor's Note: *The following is a Pascal program on fractals from two superb high school students studying under a superb teacher in Middle America. Doesn't it make you feel good?*

—Irwin Hoffman

Simple structures can arise from the most complex of processes. The study of growth dynamics and other related complex natural phenomenon reflects the essence of this statement. Inherent to nearly all growth-related patterns, such as the crystallization of solids, bacterial growth, the formations of a zinc cluster, and the pattern of an electrical discharge, is an underlying random nature, which for years has hindered many scientists in their attempts for such understanding. However, upon closer observation, a fundamental structure appears beneath the superficial chaotic exterior. Through the utilization of a computer model, we have successfully demonstrated this as an accurate explanation of specific forms of growth.

The computer model we used was a simple, mechanical approach for simulating growth. The simulation entails the release of an arbitrary number of particles guided toward the center, each released one at a time. During discrete time intervals, each particle moves randomly, with the restriction that the new distance from the origin must be less than $(1 + \Omega)$ multiplied by the original distance from the origin, where Ω is a tolerance factor independently chosen by the user. Thus, as the value of Ω becomes greater, the individual particle is allowed more freedom of movement. However, as large Ω values result in more random movements, practical time constraints become readily apparent. A value of Ω that is too large could result in infinite random movement by a single particle.

A particle is allowed to move in this fashion until it touches another existing particle, at which time this particle's movement stops. A new particle is subsequently released and undergoes a similar iteration. A seed is initially placed at the origin, in the center of the screen, in order to anchor the resultant picture. Thus, the picture is formed.

The accompanying pictures demonstrate the results of different Ω values. (See **Figure 1**.) The different growths display the effects of Ω on structure, while the tolerance information graphically displays the number of possible moves in different regions of the screen, again based on the value of Ω. ❑

```
Program Fractal Growth:
($N+)   (*Numeric Coprocessor Support*)

(* A demonstration of the resultant graphic formation based on a finite *)
(* series of random collisions, separated by apparent age of each        *)
(* generation, differentiated by sequential coloring.                    *)

    Uses
        Dos, Crt, Graph;

    Type
        ScrMtrx                       =                   Array[0..320,0..175] of Boolean;

    Var
        Mtrx                      :                   ScrMtrx;
        LX,LY,X,II,JJ             :                   Integer;
        Y,Col,Counter             :                   Integer;
        Colors,Points,GrDriver    :                   Integer;
        GrMode,OrigX,OrigY        :                   Integer;
        Touching                  :                   Boolean;
        Tol                       :                   Extended;

(*************************************  Procedures  **************************************************)

Procedure GTol;
begin
    Write('Enter Tolerance Value (0,1]: ');
    Readln(Tol);
    Write('Enter Number of Colors [1,8]: ');
    Readln(Colors);
    Write('Enter Number of Points Per Color: ');
    Readln(Points)
end;            (* GTol *)


(***************************************************************************************************************)




Procedure Tialize;
begin
    GrDriver:=Detect;
    Initgraph(GrDriver,GrMode,' ');
    Setcolor(White);
    Mtrx[160,87]:=True;
    Line(320,175,320,175)
end;        (* Initialize *)

(*********************************************************)

Procedure GivePoint;
begin
    X:=Random(316)+3; LX:=X;
    Y:=Random(171)+3; LY:=Y;
    Mtrx[X,Y]:=True
end;        (* GivePoint *)

(*******************************************************)

Procedure RanMove;
Var
    I,J          :    Integer;
    Dist,Dist2   :    Extended;

begin
    LX:=X;
    LY:=Y;
    Dist:=Sqrt(Sqr(Abs(88–Y))+Sqr(Abs(X–160)));
    I:=Random(8)+1;
```

FIGURE 1. FRACTAL PATTERNS RESULTING FROM DIFFERENT Ω VALUES.

```
Case I of
    1:  If (X>2) and (Y<173) then
            begin:
                X:=X–1;
                Y:=Y+1
            end;
    2:  If Y<173 then Y:=Y+1;
    3:  If (X<318) and (Y<173) then
            begin
                X:=X+1;
                Y:=Y+1;
            end;
    4:  If X<318 then X:=X+1;
    5:  If X>2 then X:=X–1;
    6:  If (X>2) and (Y>2) then
            begin
                X:=X–1;
                Y:=Y–1
            end;
    7:  If Y>2 then Y:=Y–1;
    8:  If (X<318) and (Y>2) then
            begin
                X:=X+1;
                Y:=Y–1
            end;
    end; (*Case*)

    Dist2:=Sqrt(Sqr(Abs(88–Y))+Sqr(Abs(X–160)));
    If Dist2>=(1+Tol)*Dist
        then begin
            X:=LX;
            Y:=LY
        end;
end; (*RanMove*)

(***********************************************************)

Procedure Draw;
begin
    If Counter=Points then
        begin
            Col:=Col+1;
            Counter:=0
        end;
            Mtrx[LX,LY]:=False;
            Mtrx[X,Y]:=True;
            Putpixel (160+LX,88+LY,Black);
            Putpixel(160+X,88+Y,Col)
end; (* Draw *)

(***********************************************************)

Procedure Check;
    begin
        If  (Mtrx[X+1,Y])
            or (Mtrx[X+1,Y+1]) or (Mtrx[X,Y+1]) or
            (Mtrx[X–1,Y+1]) or (Mtrx[X–1,Y]) or
            (Mtrx[X–1,Y–1]) or (Mtrx[X,Y–1]) or
            (Mtrx[X+1,Y–1])
            then Touching:=true
    end;    (*Check*)
(***********************************************************)

begin (* main *)
    clrscr;
    GoToI;
    GrDriver:=Detect;
    Initgraph(grDriver,GrMode, ' ');
        For II:=0 to 320 do
            For JJ:=0 to 175 do
                Mtrx[II,JJ]:=False;
    Tialize;
    Touching:=False;
    Col:=1;
    Counter:=0;
        Repeat
            Touching:=False;
            Counter:=Counter+1;
            GivePoint;
            Draw;
            Check;
            While not Touching do
                begin
                    RanMove;
                    Draw;
                    Check;
                end
        Until Keypressed or (Col=(Colors+1));
    Readln;Readln;
    Textmode(c80)
End. (* Main*)
```

WINTER 1988

TONI CARROLL
VICKI LUIBRAND

Turkey Day Child Sorting

Did you ever have the experience of celebrating Thanksgiving at a large gathering of your relatives and not being able to sort out all the children? Here is a way to sort them by age. The method assumes that if you sit comfortably on the couch or in the only vibrating easy chair or next to the dish of mints and nuts, all the kids will pass you at some time in the evening. In order to construct the sorting tree, you need only ask each one a few questions about their relative age. We have found that if the child is too young to answer personally, a nearby proud parent or aunt is eager to assist with such scholarly research and contributes the needed response.

In order to proceed logically, some rules need to be imposed. First, you need to decide that no two of the children can be the same age. Even twins have to come into the world in some order.

The sorting method uses a tree structure for sorting. Trees are structures made up of a root or base node (which may be empty) and branches, which lead to more trees (see **Figure 1**). Construct the tree according to the following rules.

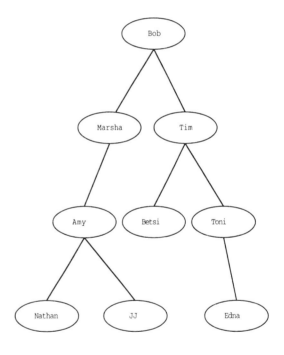

FIGURE 1. EXECUTION OF THE SORT.

Step 1   <Marsha>, Bob, <Tim>
Step 2   <Amy>, Marsha, Bob, Betsi, Tim, <Toni>
Step 3   Nathan, Amy, JJ, Marsha, Bob, Betsi, Tim, Toni, Edna

TREE-BUILDING ALGORITHM

1. If the current node of the tree is empty, then insert the child there.

2. If the current node contains child x and the child to be inserted is the same as x, then do nothing, because this just means someone has come around a second (or third) time for nuts.

3. Otherwise, compare the child to be inserted with child x stored at the current node.

   a. If $y < x$, then insert y into the left subtree by going through the algorithm from the top concentrating on this left subtree.

   b. Otherwise, insert y into the right subtree by going through the algorithm from the top concentrating on the right subtree.

4. Look for a new child to include. When you are reasonably certain that you have observed all the children, perform the following sorting algorithm.

TREE-SORTING ALGORITHM FOR RETRIEVING NAMES

1. If the tree is empty, then do nothing.

2. Otherwise, retrieve the children's names in the left subtree, then the child's name at the current node, then the children's names in the right subtree.

3. Continue resolving trees until an ordering is obtained.

The resulting list will contain all the children's names in the order of their birth, due of course to the miracle of discrete mathematics and the brilliance of your scholarly research methods! Try this on Thanksgiving day and impress your relatives.

Better yet, let a computer do the tree structure and sorting for you. The following gives the source code for a Pascal program that lets you input the children and their ages. The program then constructs the tree and sorts it using a stack data structure. To use this program as is, you need Turbo Pascal. The user does not see the underlying binary tree structure that produces the sorted list of children by age. ❏

THE SOURCE CODE FOR A PASCAL PROGRAM THAT LETS YOU INPUT
THE CHILDREN AND THEIR AGES

```pascal
PROGRAM Kids;

(* This program places children's names and ages into an
inorder tree, and prints their names out from youngest to
oldest.*)

TYPE
    Word = String[10];
    Number = 1..16;
    Component = RECORD
                    Name: Word;
                    Age: Number
                END;
    Treepointer = ^TreeNode;
    TreeNode = RECORD
                    Childs: Component;
                    Left,
                    Right: TreePointer
               END;
    StackPointer = ^StackElement;
    StackElement = RECORD
                    Element: TreePointer;
                    Link: StackPointer
                   END;
VAR
    Tree:    (* Tree of children *)
        TreePointer;
(*••••••••••••••••••••••••••••••••••••••••••••••••••••••••*)
FUNCTION TreeIsEmpty (T: Treepointer): Boolean;

(* Tests if the tree is empty *)

BEGIN (* TreeIsEmpty *)
    TreeIsEmpty := (T = NIL)
END;  (*TreeIsEmpty*)
(*••••••••••••••••••••••••••••••••••••••••••••••••••••••••*)
PROCEDURE MakeNode (VAR T: TreePointer;
                         Item: Component);

(* Creates the first node of the tree *)

BEGIN  (* MakeNode *)
    New (T);
    T^.Childs := Item;
    T^.Left := NIL;
    T^.Right := NIL
END; (* MakeNode *)
(*••••••••••••••••••••••••••••••••••••••••••••••••••••••••*)
PROCEDURE InsertNode (VAR T:TreePointer;
                          Item: Component);
(* Inserts the child's name and age into the tree *)

VAR
    Oldest:  (* First born of children the same age *)
        Word;
BEGIN (* InsertNode *)
    IF TreeIsEmpty (T) THEN
        MakeNode (T, Item)
    ELSE IF Item.Age < T^.Childs.Age THEN
        InsertNode (T^.Left, Item)
    ELSE IF Item.Age > T^.Childs.Age THEN
        InsertNode (T^.Right, Item)
    ELSE IF Item.Name <> T^.Childs.Name THEN
        BEGIN  (* Children same age *)
            Write (' Who was born first--',Item.Name,' or
            ',T^.
```

```pascal
            Childs.Name,' ? ');
            Readln (Oldest);
            IF Oldest = Item.Name THEN
                InsertNode (T^.Right, Item)
            ELSE InsertNode (T^.Left, Item)
        END (* Children same age *)
END; (* InsertNode *)
(*••••••••••••••••••••••••••••••••••••••••••••••••••••••••*)
PROCEDURE GetData (VAR Tree: TreePointer);

(* Collects the names and ages of the children and puts
them in a tree *)

VAR
    Childs:  (* The name and age read in *)
        Component;

BEGIN  (* GetData *)
    ClrScr;
    Window(15,5,65,11);
    TextColor(Yellow);
    TextBackground(Brown);
    ClrScr;
    Gotoxy(12,2);
    Writeln ('Program by Vicki Luibrand');
    Writeln;
    Writeln (' Is it time to pick names for Christmas
        presents?');
    Writeln (' Perhaps we should put the kids in order.
        We do');
    Writeln (' not want to leave anyone out, do we?');
    Writeln;
    Write (' Press the ENTER key to begin.');
    Readln;
    ClrScr;
    Gotoxy(10,2);
    Writeln ('Type "Q" for name, to quit.');
    Writeln;
    Write (' Name? ');
    Readln (Childs.Name);
    IF Childs.Name = 'Q' THEN
        Tree := NIL  (* Make tree empty *)
    ELSE
        BEGIN  (* Put names and ages in tree *)
            Write (' Age? ');
            Readln (Childs.Age);
            MakeNode (Tree, Childs);
            ClrScr;
            Gotoxy(10,2);
            Writeln ('Type "Q" for name, to quit.');
            Writeln;
            Write (' Name? ');
            Readln (Childs.name)
            WHILE Childs.Name <> 'Q' DO
                BEGIN
                    Write (' Age? ');
                    Readln (Childs.Age);
                    MakeNode (Tree, Childs);
                    ClrScr;
                    Gotoxy(10,2);
                    Writeln ('Type "Q" for name, to quit.');
                    Writeln;
                    Write (' Name? ');
                    Readln (Childs.name)
                END
        END  (* Put names and ages in tree *)
END; (* GetData *)
```

```
(***********************************************************)
FUNCTION StackIsEmpty (S: StackPointer): Boolean;

(* Tests to see if the stack is empty *)

BEGIN  (* StackIsEmpty *)
   StackIsEmpty := (S = NIL)
END;  (* StackIsEmpty *)
(***********************************************************)
PROCEDURE Initialize (VAR S: StackPointer);

(* Creates an empty stack *)

BEGIN  (* Initialize *)
   S := NIL
END;  (* Initialize *)
(***********************************************************)
PROCEDURE Push (VAR S: StackPointer;(* Pointer to top
of stack *)
Item:  TreePointer (* Tree node ptr. being pushed *))

(* Puts the node onto a stack *)

VAR
   NewNode:  (* New node to put on top of stack *)
      StackPointer;

BEGIN (* Push *)
   New (NewNode);
   NewNode^.Element := Item;
   NewNode^.Link := S;
   S := NewNode
END; (* Push *)
(***********************************************************)
PROCEDURE Pop (VAR S: StackPointer;
               VAR Item:  TreePointer);

(* Takes the next youngest child off the stack *)

VAR
   TempPointer:  (* Pointer being removed from stack *)
      StackPointer;

BEGIN (* Pop *)
   TempPointer := S;
   Item := S^.Element;
   S := S^.Link;
   Dispose (TempPointer)
END;   (* Pop *)
```

```
(***********************************************************)
PROCEDURE Print (T:  TreePointer);

(* Prints out the names of the children from youngest to
   oldest *)

VAR
   Stack:  (* Pointer to stack being built from the tree *)
      StackPointer;
   Current: (* Temporary pointer for traversing the tree *)
      TreePointer;BEGIN (* Print *)
   IF NOT TreeIsEmpty(T) THEN
      BEGIN
         Window(15,5,65,20);
         TextColor(Yellow);
         TextBackground(Brown);
         ClrScr;
         Gotoxy(10,2);
         Writeln ('Children from youngest to oldest:');
         Initialize (Stack);
         Current := T;
         REPEAT
            WHILE Current <> NIL DO
               BEGIN (* Move to far left *)
                  Push (Stack, Current);
                  Current := Current^Left
               END; (* Move left *)
            IF NOT StackIsEmpty (Stack) THEN
            BEGIN (* Print and move to right subtree *)
               Pop (Stack, Current);
               Writeln (' ',Current^.Childs.Name);
               Current := Current^.Right
            END; (* Move right *)
         UNTIL (Current = NIL) AND (StackIsEmpty
            (Stack));
         Gotoxy(10,2);
         Window(1,1,80,25)
      END (* IF NOT TreeIsEmpty *)
   ELSE
      Writeln (' There are no children in your family?')
END; (* Print *)
(***********************************************************)
BEGIN (* Kids *)
   GetData (Tree);
   Print (Tree)
END. (* Kids *)
```

SUMMER 1987

PAULA POTTER
CHRIS DOEHLER

Getting in the Swing of Things

Simple Harmonic Motion

As a high school mathematics teacher, I am always looking for creative ways to model specific mathematical concepts. Not all students learn best from teacher-oriented formal lecture format; concrete models can bring math to life. The following presentation was accomplished by one of my trigonometry students, Chris Doehler. Recognizing his computer talents, I sought to challenge him in both fields by requesting that he design for my trigonometry class an example of simple harmonic motion: the classic swinging pendulum. I wanted my students to simultaneously view both the pendulum in motion and an accompanying graph representing this motion as a function of time.

While the demonstration was not particularly unique, it did accomplish what I anticipated. The transfer of learning progressed from simply graphing sine waves to recognizing that sine waves express all periodic movements that occur in the real world. Chris's observation was insightful as well. When he began the project, he thought of it as a mathematical problem. Once in process, he realized that there were other considerations: Mathematics in action became applied science. It was a learning experience for all.

Physicists *know* that ideally a pendulum is *not* a simple harmonic oscillator. Therefore, this is a rough model that none-the-less gives students a "feel" for the concept. Keep in mind, an *initial* mathematical model is just that! It has been noted that the lengthening of the period is due not to friction but to the failure of the return force on the mass m to be proportional to the angular displacement θ, unless $|\theta| \leq 1$ radian (based on comments by Frank E. Rose, Dept. of Physics, Univ. of Michigan). (See **Figure 1.**)

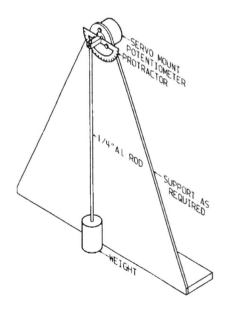

FIGURE 1. THE SETUP OF THE PENDULUM.

Here lies a great opportunity for an interdisciplinary unit in which forces affecting the pendulum can be explained mathematically and physically. For alternative means of modeling harmonic motion, the IBM Personal Science Laboratory, using both the rotary motion and distance probe, can examine harmonic motion easily by simply using a vibrating ruler. ❏

Paula Potter
Berthoud High School
Berthoud, CO

I was asked by my trigonometry teacher to plot the motion of a pendulum using a computer. After considering many approaches, both mine and those suggested to me, I discussed the assignment with my computer teacher and decided on the following method (shown in **Figures 2** and **4**).

With this method, a 10,000 ohm potentiometer serves as the pivot for the pendulum, and the motion of the pendulum causes a change in resistance to be read by the computer. The data enter the computer by way of the games port, very similar to the way game paddles and joysticks work. Pin 1 (5 vdc) of the games port is attached to one contact on the potentiometer. The other contact is connected to pin 3, which allows the computer to read the resistance in the potentiometer. The resistance level is then converted into a decimal between 0 and 255. This number can be accessed by using the STICK function in the BASIC programming language (see lines 140, 220, 260, and 320 in Figure 4).

The program uses the numbers read by the STICK function and converts them to y-coordinate numbers, which, when plotted, create a sine wave. Lines 100 through 140 find the y-coordinate level when the pendulum is at rest. Lines 200 through 270 make the computer wait until the pendulum is raised and then released. Data are gathered by lines

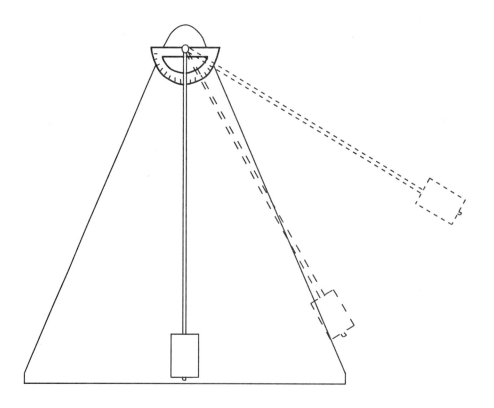

FIGURE 2. The swinging pendulum.

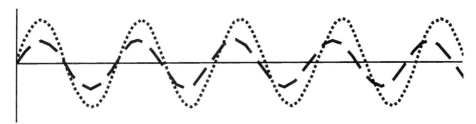

FIGURE 3. 30° DISPLACEMENT VS. 60° DISPLACEMENT.

300 through 340 after the pendulum passes the 0 degrees mark. As the computer gets the 640 *y*-coordinates, it plots them on screen. Lastly, in lines 900 through 980, there is the option of superimposing graphs or starting new ones. (Superimposition comes in handy when comparing the frequency of waves of different amplitudes.)

This project looked foolproof on paper, but as in most cases, if something seems too good to be true, it probably is. Basic laws of physics state that pendulums with the same lengths but different amplitudes will have the same frequencies. However, this is only true in a frictionless environment. As you can see in **Figure 3**, the amplitude of the wave slightly affects the frequency because of the friction in the potentiometer. Though this project is not a good demonstration of precise math and physics laws, it is an excellent example of how our environment affects the laws of science. ❏

Chris Doehler
Berthoud High School
Berthoud, CO 80501
(currently a student at MIT).

```
10 REM ********* PLOT MOTION OF PENDULUM *********
99 :
100 REM *** FIND RESISTANCE VALUE WHEN
    PENDULUM IS AT REST ***
110 CLS:SCREEN 2:KEY OFF
120 LOCATE 1,1:PRINT "IS THE PENDULUM AT THE
    ZERO DEGREE MARK :";
130 IF INKEY$<>"Y" THEN 130
140 ZEROX=STICK (0)
150 :
200 REM *** MAKE COMPUTER WAIT UNTIL PENDULUM
    IS RAISED AND RELEASED AGAIN ***
210 LOCATE 1,1:PRINT "GRAPHING WILL BEGIN AFTER
    PENDULUM IS RAISED TO DESIRED HEIGHT AND
    RELEASED."
220 IF STICK (0)=ZEROX THEN 220
230 LOCATE 1,1:PRINT SPACE$(80)
240 LOCATE 1,35:PRINT "WAITING"
250 LINE (0,100) -(640,100):LINE (0,40) -(0,160)
260 IF STICK (0)<>ZEROX THEN 260
270 PSET (0,100):LOCATE 1,35:PRINT "ACQUIRING
    DATA"
280 :
300 REM *** GET DATA AND PLOT IT ***
310 FOR X=1 TO 640
320 Y=100+(1.5*(ZEROX-STICK (0)))
330 LINE -(X,Y)
340 NEXT X
350 :
900 REM *** PLAY IT AGAIN, SAM? ***
910 LOCATE 1,35:PRINT "DONE"
920 LOCATE 22,1:PRINT "PRESS SPACE TO CONTINUE
OR ANY OTHER KEY TO END."
930 ANS$=INKEY$:IF ANS$=" " THEN 930
940 IF ANS$<>" " THEN END
950 LOCATE 22,1:PRINT "PRESS SPACE TO
    SUPERIMPOSE OR ANY OTHER KEY FOR NEW
    SCREEN."
960 ANS$=INKEY$:IF ANS$=" " THEN 960
970 IF ANS$<>" " THEN CLS ELSE LOCATE 22,1:PRINT
    SPACE$(79)
980 GOTO 120
990 :
```

FIGURE 4. CHRIS'S BASIC PROGRAM.

WINTER 1987

FRANK E. ROSE

Pendulum Period Variation

Amplitude or Friction?

The previous article by Chris Doehler reported on an excellent job of interfacing a real pendulum to a computer. The angular displacement of the pendulum is then displayed in a graph versus time, t. Although it is true that a simple harmonic oscillator is isochronous (i.e., has a period—the time interval required for one oscillation—that is unaffected by the angular amplitude of its motion), physicists know that a pendulum is not generally a simple harmonic oscillator.

The period, T, of a simple pendulum having a fixed length, L, is related to its angular amplitude, θ (its maximum angular displacement), as follows.

$$T = 2\pi[L/g] [1 + (1/4) \sin^2 (\theta/2) + (9/64) \sin^4 (\theta/2) + \ldots], \quad \textbf{(1)}$$

where g is the acceleration of gravity [Sears, Young, and Zemansky 1985, 232].

If one thinks briefly about the physics involved, one will realize that the period of a given oscillating pendulum is not a constant but must increase with amplitude. Consider an idealized ("simple") pendulum having a bob of mass m, suspended on a rigid rod of negligible mass. When m swings upward to an angle of nearly 180° above plumb, it nearly gets stuck, so this pendulum then has a greatly increased period.

If θ is small, then the pendulum's period is $T_0 + 2\pi [L/g]$; it is isochronous. But for $\theta = 30°$ (the smaller amplitude used for the graph that was published), then the simple harmonic period T_0 needs to be increased by

$$0.25 \sin^2 (15°) = 1/57 = 1.74\%.$$

So, 57 periods at an amplitude of 30° would require as much time as would 58 periods at a very small amplitude, say, 2°.

However, an amplitude of 60° requires a period correction over four times that at 30°, that is, 7.1%. Accordingly, the fractional difference between the time required for any given number of oscillations is $(7.1 - 1.7)\%$, or approximately 5%, as is consistent with the published graph of the actual experimental data captured by the computer. Also, on the graph, four 60° oscillations appear to require 1.05 times as long as the time interval required for four oscillations at $\theta = 30°$.

It is true that friction can measurably increase the period of a coasting pendulum. However, in such cases, a decrease in the amplitude would become apparent to a viewer much more readily than would an increase in period. The amplitude would include a decaying exponential factor: exp[–*Gt*], where *G* (the "damping factor") rises from zero as friction increases [Symon 1971].

The graph in **Figure 1** that is plotted for θ = 60° exhibits a period that is approximately *S* ≡ 7% above that for a very small amplitude, as is consistent with the non-small-amplitude equation in **(1)** for *T*. However, if this increase in period had been the result of friction, how severely would the amplitude be expected to decrease in just one oscillation? The answer requires an evaluation of *Gt* for *t* = *T*.

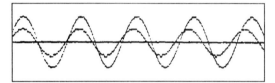

FIGURE 1. 30° DISPLACEMENT VERSUS 60° DISPLACEMENT. THE GRAPH REPRINTED FROM *CONSORTIUM* 22.

The theoretical mechanics of a coasting, frictionally damped, oscillato (e.g., the real pendulum being studied) relates the actual period, *T*, to the undamped period, T_0, by

$$1/T^2 = 1/T_0{}^2 - (G/2\pi)2, \text{ or}$$
$$(GT/2\pi)^2 = [(T + T_0)/\ T_0]\ [(T - T_0)/T_0].$$

For *T* not much more than T_0, the first [ ] is approximately 2. The second [ ] is just *S*. Substitute these values algebraically to get

$$GT + 2\pi(2S)^{1/2}.$$

Substitution of *S* = 0.07 gives *GT* = +2.3, approximately.

Consider the one oscillation that starts when the displacement first reaches its maximum (the amplitude). This requires one period of time, *T*. During this period, the amplitude would be expected to be multiplied by the factor exp[–*GT*] = exp[–2.3] = 1/10, approximately. During each period, the amplitude would be expected to decrease by 90%, to 0.1 of its value at the beginning of that cycle of oscillation.

No such corresponding decrease in amplitude is found in the graph, although such an associated decrease would need to occur if the increase in period had been caused by friction.

Clearly, the lengthening of the period arises not from friction, but rather from the failure of the return force on *m* to be proportional to the angular displacement, φ, except for |φ| ~ 1 radian. (See **Figure 2**.) In fact, after dividing the force by *m* and by *L*, the acceleration of φ is found to be $-(g/L)^{1/2}\sin\phi$. At small amplitudes, this becomes $-(g/L)^{1/2}\phi$. So the oscillator becomes isochronous if the maximum value of φ is small (e.g., if θ ~ 1 radian). ❑

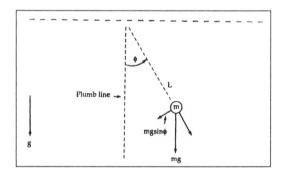

FIGURE 2. THE AUTHOR'S EXPLANATION.

Frank E. Rose
Dept. of Physics
Univ. of Michigan—Flint
Flint, MI 48501-2186

REFERENCES

Doehler, Chris. 1987. Simple harmonic motion. *Consortium* 22:(May); 10.

Sears, Francis W., Hugh D. Young, and Mark W. Zemansky. 1985. *College Physics*. 6th ed. Reading, MA: Addison-Wesley Publishing Company.

Symon, K. 1971. *Mechanics*. 3d ed. Reading, MA: Addison-Wesley Publishing Company.

WINTER 1988

JO ANN FELLIN, OSB

Base Conversion

In this computer age, it is much easier to see the application of nondecimal number bases than in the "new math" era when number base conversion appeared as a topic either for enrichment or as an aid to a better understanding of the familiar decimal system. In particular, today it is not difficult to convince ourselves that base 2 is important. We need only reflect on the two-fold aspect of current (on, off) in computing technology.

BASE CONVERSION MORE THAN ENRICHMENT

The concept of "algorithm" has been enlarged for us by technology and will most likely continue to become more important. We can no longer think merely of a method for performing an arithmetic operation. If we are going to program a computer to do a task, we are led to consider not only a method but which method can be coded most easily for the machine calculation.

In this article, we reflect on the method of converting a base 10 numeral to its base 2 representation. The discussion can be generalized to conversion from base 10 to any arbitrary base B less than 10. We confine our remarks throughout to positive integer conversion.

HOW DO *YOU* CHANGE FROM BASE 10 TO BASE 2?

At this point, you may wish to suspend reading the remainder of the article until you have reflected on how you, yourself, change 54, (base 10) to 110110 (base 2).

Did you start subtracting off the highest power of 2 possible, i.e., 54 − 32 = 22? Continuing in this manner, 54 = 32 + 16 + 4 + 2. The bits are supplied from left to right to obtain 110110 (base 2).

Did you divide 54 by the highest power of 2 that goes into 54, namely 32, and then divide the remainder, 22, by the highest power of 2 that goes into 22 and so on—supplying the bits (the quotients of the divisions) from left to right?

Or rather did you arrive at the bits of base-2 representation from the rightmost bit to the leftmost bit by a division by 2 process? Dividing 54 by 2, the remainder is the "units" bit, namely 0. The new quotient, 27, divided by 2, has remainder 1, the 2's bit. Continuing this process, we supply the bits (the remainders of the divisions) from right to left. It is this procedure that we will discuss here—a "right to left" procedure, which the author prefers. We contend that this procedure has the greater applicability for computing—it introduces two operators, namely DIV and MOD, useable in other programming tasks and it provides an algorithm that is easier to program.

COUNTING THE NUMBER OF DIGITS/BITS

Let us digress now to a consideration of counting the number of digits in the representation of a positive integer as a numeral. This is not a necessary digression but will motivate the algorithm we intend to present for base conversion.

First let us consider determining the number of digits in the decimal numeral 5427. The decimal representation on division by 10 is 542.7—the quotient part being 542. If we continue dividing the new quotient by 10 until the quotient finally becomes 0, we can determine the number of digits by establishing a counter that increases the count at the completion of each division.

The DIV operator is a convenient way to denote the quotient, e.g., 5427 DIV 10 is 542. If we denote the count by the integer j, then j is 1 after the first division is completed.

Execute the program in **Figure 1** to see that the variable NumberOfDigits is assigned 4 when the input for N is 5427, the input for Base is 10, and j is set initially to 0. (Note that ":=" is used to denote that a variable is assigned a certain value.) The intermediate results are displayed in **Table 1**.

```
repeat
    N := N DIV Base;
    j := j + 1;
until N = 0;
    Number Of Digits := j;

input: N = 5427 Base = 10
```

Figure 1. The base conversion Pascal program.

Table 1. Output of NumberOfDigits.

after execution	quotient	count
first	542	$j = 1$
second	54	2
third	5	3
fourth	0	4

output: NumberOfDigits = 4

Examine the program in Figure 1 to see how it works for a base other than 10, say for $N = 54$ and Base = 2. We know 54 (base 10) = 110110 (base 2). This algorithm produces 6 for the NumberOfDigits (called *bits*) of the base-2 representation of 54. In base conversion, though, we desire the actual bits, not just the number of bits.

RIGHT-TO-LEFT METHOD FOR BASE CONVERSION

We consider again the decimal number 5427. Division by 10 separates the numeral into two distinct parts separated by the decimal point—the quotient part to the left (542), and the remainder part to the right (7). We denoted the quotient part with the DIV operator. The remainder part is the "units" digit, which we denote with the MOD operator, namely 5427 MOD 10 is 7; i.e., the remainder when 5427 is divided by 10 is 7. If we take the next quotient, 542, and apply the MOD operator, we obtain the "tens" digit of the original 5427 numeral, i.e., 542 MOD 10 is 2. Repeating this process until we have reached the NumberOfDigits number will produce the digits from the right to the left. Execute the program in **Figure 2** to verify the digit entries displayed in **Table 2**.

```
q := NumberOfDigits (N, Base);
for i := 1 to q do
    begin
        digit(i) := N MOD Base;
        N := N DIV Base
end
```

Figure 2. A Pascal program to verify the digit entries in Table 2.

TABLE 2.

For $N = 5427$ and Base $= 10$, $q = 4$;

	remainder			quotient	
digit(1) = 5427	MOD 10 = 7	5427	DIV 10 = 542
digit(2) = 542	MOD 10 = 2	542	DIV 10 = 54
digit(3) = 54	MOD 10 = 4	54	DIV 10 = 5
digit(4) = 5	MOD 10 = 5	5	DIV 10 = 0

Applying the algorithm for $N = 54$, Base $= 2$, and $q = 6$, we find

TABLE 3.

	remainder		quotient
digit(1) = 54	MOD 2 = 0	54 DIV 2 = 27
digit(2) = 27	MOD 2 = 1	27 DIV 2 = 13
digit(3) = 13	MOD 2 = 1	13 DIV 2 = 6
digit(4) = 6	MOD 2 = 0	6 DIV 2 = 3
digit(5) = 3	MOD 2 = 1	3 DIV 2 = 1
digit(6) = 1	MOD 2 = 1	1 DIV 2 = 0

We place the bits from right to left (top to bottom in **Table 3**) to form the binary representation of 54, namely 110110 (base 2). Essentially this process involves dividing a number by 2 at each stage—an easier process than speculating regarding the highest power of 2 that divides the number as was done in the "left to right" process.

It may be apparent now, after working with the algorithm, that the q-value (the number of digits) indicates when the procedure terminates. This value is used only as an aid in programming and need not be introduced.

Thus the "right-to-left" method for base conversion is accomplished by successive divisions by the base. The digit entries are established from right to left—the digit entries are the remainders upon these successive divisions. The procedure terminates when the quotient becomes 0.

JUSTIFICATION FOR THE RIGHT-TO-LEFT METHOD

If we consider the number written as a sum of powers of 2, e.g., $54 = 32 + 16 + 4 + 2$, then the terms "right to left" and "left to right" could indicate merely the direction we use in supplying the bits to display the base-2 representation. But suppose the number is not given as a sum of powers of 2. We now justify the "right to left" procedure of taking the remainders after successive divisions to obtain the bits from right to left for the base-2 representation. Why does the method work?

We illustrate the justification with 54. The following equation given by the division algorithm when dividing 54 by 2 clearly shows both the first quotient and the first remainder:

$$54 = (27)2 + \underline{0} = (q_1)2 + r_1$$

We now apply the division algorithm to the first quotient, q_1, and obtain:

$$54 = ([13]2 + \underline{1})2 + \underline{0} = ([q_2]2 + r_2)2 + r_1$$

Continuing in this manner, we obtain:

$$54 = ([[[([0]2 + \underline{1})2 + \underline{1}]2 + \underline{0})2 + \underline{1}]2 + \underline{1})2 + \underline{0}.$$

(Note that the last quotient is 0.) For clarity, the remainders are underlined. Using the distributive property and performing the multiplications from inside out, we again have 54 written as a sum of powers of 2, namely:

$$54 = \underline{1}(2^5) + \underline{1}(2^4) + \underline{0}(2^3) + \underline{1}(2^2) + \underline{1}(2) + \underline{0}.$$

Thus, we see that on successive divisions by 2, the remainders are the bit entries of the base-2 representation of 54.

Let us compare the justification of this "right-to-left" procedure with a justification of the division process that supplies the bits from left to right. We shall again illustrate with 54. From the division by the highest power of 2 dividing 54, we obtain the equation: (quotient underlined)

$$54 = \underline{1}(32) + 22.$$

Now we break down the remainder 22 and obtain:

$$54 = \underline{1}(32) + \underline{1}(16) + 6.$$

Continuing in this manner, we have:

$$54 = \underline{1}(32) + \underline{1}(16) + \underline{1}(4) + \underline{1}(2).$$

Thus, 54 (base 10) = 110110(base 2).

Setting these methods side-by-side as follows:

"right-to-left" bits supplied by quotients	"left-to-right" bits supplied by remainders

$$(27)2 + \underline{0} = 54 = \underline{1}(32) + 22$$
$$([13]2 + \underline{1})2 + \underline{0} = 54 = \underline{1}(32) + \underline{1}(16) + 6$$
$$\cdots$$
$$([[[([0]2 + \underline{1})2 + \underline{1}]2$$
$$+ \underline{0})2 + \underline{1}]2 + \underline{1})2$$
$$+ \underline{0} = 54 = \underline{1}(32) + \underline{1}(16)$$
$$+ \underline{1}(4) + \underline{1}(2),$$

we see that while the justification of the "right to left" procedure may at first appear more complex, it really is not on closer examination.

CONCLUSION

The "right to left" procedure involves a simpler process at each stage—division by 2. The zero bits appear in the "right to left" procedure, whereas in the "left to right," the zero bits must be supplied wherever a power of 2 is missing in the representation. Furthermore, the "right to left" procedure is easier to code for machine calculation since it doesn't involved speculation on the highest power of 2 that will divide a number. ❑

FALL 1988

PAULA POTTER
BARRY EPPLER

Expand Your Curriculum
Include Mathematical Modeling

Editor's Note: *Paula teaches in a rural farm community in Colorado. What an exciting experience for her students to have a Woodrow Wilson Scholar and an engineer direct their explorations. More rural communities should be provided these experiences.*

The IBM Personal Science Laboratory can be used to measure volume of air in a balloon if the balloon is almost perfectly round. To do so, use the distance probe mounted sufficiently above the balloon being inflated from below. By measuring the resulting distance, the diameter and subsequently the volume of the spherical balloon can be computed.

I am always searching for ways to make mathematics come to life in the classroom. This search led to the following illustration of mathematical modeling where a graph became a model and computer graphics aided in adding insight to a relatively simple concept. It has been eight years since the NCTM Agenda for Action indicated that problem solving should be the focus of mathematics education in the 1980s. What impact does that have on a high-school mathematics program already bursting from a demanding curriculum?

We are not developing a nation of better problem-solvers merely by assigning more word problems or applications from the text, although such assignments are important in order to show relevance. Students given such problems typically determine the mathematics necessary to solve the problem and arrive at the correct answer to the problem. What else can be done to truly develop better problem solvers? Experience in mathematical modeling!

Mathematical modeling is the epitome of realistic problem solving that spans across all fields of endeavors—city planning, economics, finance, and a plethora of scientific fields. A model is merely a representation of some particular phenomenon. The model is generally a simplified representation of the salient characteristics of the phenomenon. (An example of a model is a road map that approximated intersecting streets in a particular area.) The model may be a mathematical formula, an expression of a picture that reflects the phenomenon. The type of model used depends on what aspect of the problem is under investigation.

Why develop a model? Often in scientific realms, experimenting with certain factors is unrealistic or dangerous. (For example, we would not set off a nuclear explosion to study the validity of the nuclear-winter theory.) Henceforth, theoretical models are developed.

The construction of a mathematical model follows certain basic steps:

1. Identify a problem or question.
2. Build the model.
   a. Identify and classify the variables of the problem.
   b. Determine the interrelationship between the variables.
   c. Make assumptions about relevant inputs when data is not available.
3. Solve the model for the desired output.
4. Verify the model.
   a. Does it address the problem?
   b. Does it make common sense?
   c. Does it compare with real-world data (or other models)?
5. Implement the model—make predictions and/or explanations.
6. Maintain the model—reexamine the model in light of additional information.

With mathematical modeling, we are using mathematics as the vehicle or tool to aid in the understanding of a particular real-world problem, and not as an end in itself. The "new" way of thinking was explored at the Woodrow Wilson Foundation summer institute of 1987 at Princeton University. I was privileged to be among 50 math fellows to explore how various disciplines use mathematical modeling to assist in their particular field. What an exciting experience!

Back in the classroom, I was determined to provide my trigonometry students with this approach to mathematical thinking. Initially, I was exploring functional relationships and asked students to draw a "reasonable" sketch of various phenomena—in this particular instance, to sketch the relationship between the volume of air in a balloon that was being inflated over a period of time. Sketches similar to **Figure 1** were typical. Questions arose as to how much air each breath contained. Did it vary? How much air escaped each time?

I had the good fortune to work with Barry Eppler, an engineer from Hewlett-Packard in the Visiting Scientist program. After discussing

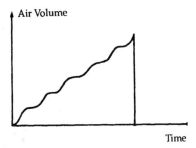

FIGURE 1. A TYPICAL STUDENT'S SKETCH.

this functional-thinking concept, we decided to expand on this idea to create some interest in mathematical modeling, with the hopes that this example would balloon (no pun intended) into even more exposure to the process of mathematical modeling.

A class day was set aside for this exercise. Using the concept of cooperative learning, students worked in small groups of four. Each student was supplied with a balloon. The directions were as follows:

1. The students were asked to draw a sketch relating the expected air pressure within a balloon as it is being blown up, using small time increments.

Again, their graphs looked almost identical to the ones drawn earlier showing volume increase.

2. The students experimented by actually blowing up their balloons and resketching the designs, if necessary.
3. Finally, Mr. Eppler hooked up an electronic measuring system and a computer to monitor the balloon inflation and bursting (see **Figure 2**). The computer printed out a graph of pressure vs. time (see **Figure 3**).

There was a considerable difference between the model that the students thought would be true and the actual situation. The students were asked to explain what factor produced such a result that they had apparently not considered earlier; what variable had they overlooked? Through class discussion, it was determined that the nature of the container

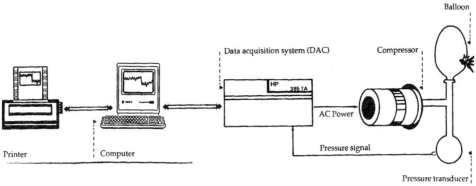

FIGURE 2. BALLOON PRESSURE MEASUREMENT APPARATUS.

(balloon) with its elastic expanding sides kept the air pressure from increasing beyond a certain level, until such time as it burst. Therefore, the model (graph) they had designed needed to be altered.

Questions arose. What predictions could be made if the sides were more rigid? What accounted for the differences in the individual model of their graphs; constant/variable air flow, constant/variable volume, strength of the balloon, etc. It was apparent to the students that the model needed to be changed to more realistically reflect what occurred.

This is a very basic example no doubt, but by doing this exercise, the students experienced active participation in mathematical modeling, which contains many of the components of real problem-solving that the NCTM Agenda for Action states students must learn to do:

- formulate key questions;
- analyze and conceptualize problems;
- define the problem and the goal;
- discover patterns and similarities;
- seek out appropriate data; and
- experiment.

The equipment and the role it played in this exercise is described by Barry Eppler in the second part of this article. ❑

Paula Potter
Berthoud High School
Berthoud, Colorado

THE TECHNICAL SIDE

The balloon modeling experience demonstrates for students how physical measurements relate to mathematical models. In this case, a computer and data-acquisition system* are used to make a physical measurement of pressure to record the phenomenon of balloon inflation and bursting. The apparatus used to make the pressure measurement is shown in Figure 2.

HOW IT WORKS

To begin the measurement, the computer instructs the data acquisition system (DAC) to turn on power to the compressor. As the balloon inflates, its internal pressure is sensed by the pressure transducer and converted to a voltage. This voltage is read repeatedly by the DAC at intervals as close as 10 μsec. When a rapid pressure drop is sensed by the DAC

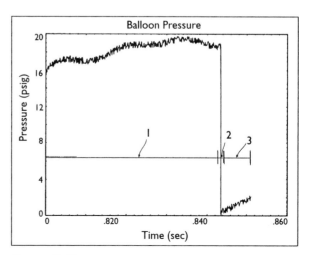

FIGURE 3. TYPICAL BALLOON INFLATION CURVE.

(indicating that the balloon has burst), the readings stored inside the DAC are transmitted to the computer. The computer then displays and prints a graph of balloon pressure vs. time.

USING THE MEASUREMENT RESULTS

Figure 3 shows a typical balloon-inflation curve. This graph is centered tightly around a balloon burst. A graph such as this serves as a standard against which students can test their models. Not only should the graphical representation of the model be compared, but the underlying assumptions, observations, and theories of the model itself should be questioned in light of the physical measurement. To assist students in comparing their models to the measured behavior, consider asking the following questions:

- What is happening in regions 1, 2, and 3 (Figure 3)? Students should be able to identify these as inflation, bursting, and after-burst periods.
- How does pressure change in regions 1, 2, and 3 and why does it change in that manner? For example, is it constant or does it change linearly?
- What is the duration of the actual burst event?
- How accurately did students predict time and pressure scales? How could observation and comparison be used to closely approximate proper scaling? For example, would a balloon burst at lower or higher pressure than a car tire that holds 30 psi?

FINDING YOUR OWN EQUIPMENT

Many high-school math teachers may find the measurement system described here too difficult to construct themselves. But do not be overwhelmed; it is not as formidable as it may appear! An experienced physics instructor, engineer, or engineering student should be able to provide the required

technical skills to operate the system. While the measurement system described here utilized relatively sophisticated instrumentation, a number of substitutions are possible.

To study pre-burst inflation, a strip chart recorder may be used, eliminating the need for both a DAC and a computer. A digital or storage oscilloscope is fast enough to study both inflation and bursting, and also eliminates the need for a DAC and computer. A pressure transducer is required regardless of the measurement device being used. An inexpensive 0-30 psig transducer should be adequate. A wide range of pressure transducers are available from Omega Engineering (One Omega Dr., Box 4047 Stamford, CT 06907) for $40-$100. Bottled gas, an air tank, a bicycle pump, or human breath may be substituted for the compressor, and each will yield unique results worth studying.

Demonstrating the physical measurement may not always be possible. In that case, consider conducting the exercise and simply present Figure 2 as a typical result. ❏

Barry Eppler
Visiting Scientist
Hewlett-Packard
Loveland, CO

REFERENCES

Foerster, Paul A. 1984. *Trigonometry: Functions and Applications*, 2nd ed. Reading, MA: Addison-Wesley Publishing Company.

NCTM. 1980. *NCTM Agenda for Action: Recommendations for School Mathematics in the 1980s.* Reston, VA: NCTM.

North Carolina School of Science and Math, 4th Year College Preparatory Mathematics course (under development). Durham, NC: NCSSM.

Section 2

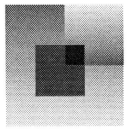

One of the most exciting software innovations in recent years is the dynamic

geometric drawing package. This section's articles demonstrate why the drawing,

measuring, and animation features of this type of software make it an effective

mathematical modeling tool. Will the future bring miniature hand-held versions of

these products as well?

FALL 1989

DEBORAH RANDOLPH

Geometry Software

Sunburst's *Geometric Supposers* and IBM's *Geometry One* and *Geometry Two*

Iigh school students often approach their first contact with the abstract mathematics of geometry seriously disadvantaged by a meager knowledge of the basic principles. It is not easy to prove that chords equidistant from the center of a circle are congruent if the student has minimal experience with the concepts "chord," or "equidistant," or "congruent." Unfortunately, elementary math programs focus briefly, if at all, on development of geometry basics.

Consequently, students are left to fill in these important gaps on their own while simultaneously struggling to understand the abstract principles of axiomatic systems and deductive reasoning. This double assignment is tough at best and has been compounded by cumbersome and limiting visual aids: the straightedge and compass.

Recently, however, the increased memory capability of personal computers, coupled with improved graphics tools and thoughtful planning, have generated mathematics software that allows students to "see" the variety of figures quickly and accurately in a way that has never before been possible. Recent mandates about the necessity for discovery learning in mathematics are finally feasible with these programs.

There are two sets of geometry software that present wonderful opportunities for guided and open-ended exploration of geometric notions. Used as an electronic blackboard, each also allows teachers to present concepts in ways not possible with traditional tools.

One is the set of products marketed by Sunburst called the *Geometric Supposers*. They were developed by Judah Schwartz and Michal Yerushalmy of the Center for Learning Technology at Education Development Center in Newton, Maine. Initial versions of the *Supposers* are about four years old.

The second set of products are those marketed by IBM, known as *Geometry One: Foundations* and *Geometry Two: Proofs and Extensions*, which became available about two years ago. They were developed for WICAT Systems by Max S. Bell of the University of Chicago.

The following comparison will focus primarily on differences between the two products. This comparison will include:

- an overview of the physical specifications of the two sets of products;
- a description of their main intent and educational focus;
- a comparison describing major features that are available in one and not the other; and
- a table of specific features and their availability in each of the products.

GEOMETRIC SUPPOSERS

OVERVIEW

There are three *Geometric Supposers* for the high-school level:

- *The Geometric Supposer Triangles;*
- *The Geometric Supposer Quadrilaterals;*
- *The Geometric Supposer Circles.*

These are separate pieces of software that run on the Apple II+, Apple IIe, and Apple IIGS with at least 64K memory and monochrome monitor. In addition, a version of *The Geometric Supposer Triangles* is available for the IBM PC/PCjr which requires 256K memory. (Some features of the *Supposers* are only available for the Apple IIGS and the IBM versions. They are discussed below.)

PRODUCT DESCRIPTION

The *Geometric Supposers* are a set of tools exploring the geometric relationships involving triangles, quadrilaterals, and circles. They duplicate constructions possible with a straightedge and compass in an enhanced way by providing consistent accuracy and rapid presentation.

A nested and clear menu structure facilitates use of the product even by beginners. A DATA column on the left-hand side of the screen records all measurements for later transfer by students to their worksheets.

A perfectly wonderful feature is the ability of the software to remember and recreate a series of constructions done on one figure for other figures. For example, one could draw all three angle bisectors for an equilateral triangle, and with just a couple of keystrokes, duplicate that sequence of commands for

scalene and isosceles triangles. (For the Apple IIGS and IBM versions only, all data measurements that had been done for the original triangle are automatically recalculated for the new figures and displayed in the DATA column.)

This REPEAT feature (available for triangles and quadrilaterals, but not for circles) allows students to truly explore geometric relationships among similar kinds of figures. It allows them to generate ideas for theorems by uncovering mathematical relationships which they can later prove.

Several publications are available separately which provide support material for the *Geometric Supposers*:

- *Geometry Problems and Projects Triangles*
  (This is a set of some 70 lab sheets with corresponding teacher notes targeting possible explorations which can be done with the *Geometric Supposers*.)
- *Geometry Problems and Projects Quadrilaterals*
- *Geometry Problems and Projects Circles*
- *Geometry: A Guided Inquiry*
  (This is a geometry textbook that introduces concept areas as guided inquiries. It does not specifically refer to the *Supposers* but it does lend itself to an integration with the *Supposer* approach.)
- *The Geometry Course Guide*
  (This is a comprehensive curriculum guide that lays out a year's course in geometry suggesting day-by-day activities which integrate the three *Supposers* with all of the above publications.)

GEOMETRY ONE/GEOMETRY TWO

OVERVIEW

There are two IBM Geometry products:
- *Geometry One: Foundations*;
- *Geometry Two: Proofs and Extensions.*

Each of these products is available on two 5.25" or one 3.5" disk for any of the IBM line of computers with at least 128K memory and a color monitor. These two pieces of software sell separately and come with basic documentation that describes the program, lesson objectives, and special suggested exercises. More extensive publication support is not required because of the well-designed and comprehensive lessons available on the software itself.

A K–8 mathematics product called *Math Concepts*, also designed by WICAT Systems and marketed by IBM, incorporates an extensive geometry strand beginning at the preschool level.

PRODUCT DESCRIPTION

Geometry One: Foundations and *Geometry Two: Proofs and Extensions* are two separate products that together provide a comprehensive course in high school geometry.

Geometry One has three graphing tools, as well as an organized set of learning activities which encourage the development of students' intuitive understanding of geometric concepts. It covers standard plane geometry propositions associated with traditional geometry courses.

The three graphing modes in *Geometry One* mirror three different approaches to geometry:

- the construction approach (CONSTRUCT);
- the transformational approach (TRANSFORM); and
- the vector approach (V-DRAW).

The CONSTRUCT mode allows typical straightedge and compass drawing. The TRANSFORM mode allows transformations such as reflections, rotations, translations, shears, and scaling on drawn figures. The V-DRAW mode, which is similar to the Logo programming language, allows students to explore geometry using vectors. It includes a DEFER option that students can use to store and execute a set of V-DRAW commands an open-ended number of times.

Geometry Two: Proofs and Extensions is a one-semester course covering the standard proof content of a typical geometry course. Students are quizzed on their understanding of the principles involved in proofs for a given section and referred to *Geometry One* if they need a better intuitive feel for concepts being proved. All three graphic modes from *Geometry One* are available to users of *Geometry Two.*

Imbedded in *Geometry Two* is a utility called PROOFCHECKER, an intelligent checking system that allows students to enter proofs in any logical manner or using any logical approach. It checks each step as well as the final proof for correctness, marking any superfluous steps. Approximately 90 proofs are included in *Geometry Two.*

CONTRASTING *THE SUPPOSERS* WITH *GEOMETRY ONE* AND *GEOMETRY TWO*

While both products do a good job of allowing students to really explore and get an intuitive feel for certain geometric concepts, each has its relative strengths. This section focuses on the major strengths each product has in comparison to the other.

The *Geometric Supposers* have four main features that are not available in *Geometry One* or *Geometry Two*. They are:

- The REPEAT feature in the *Geometric Supposers Triangles* and the *Geometric Supposer Quadrilaterals* allows the same explorations to occur automatically on a variety of figures. Conjectures about whether a given rule is valid over all figures can quickly be explored with this feature.

- The *Supposers* have a DATA column so measurements will remain on the screen (until scrolled up), allowing students to compare data results.

- There is an automatic angle bisection function. (In *Geometry One*, users must measure the angle and then draw a ray equal to half that measure.)

- The *Supposers* feature enhanced measurement capabilities. In addition to measuring lengths and angles, the *Supposers* can also measure perimeter and area. (This must be calculated from length measurements in *Geometry One*.)

- The *Supposers* will also calculate the sum, difference, product, or ratio of any two measurements and find the square of any measurement, as well.

Geometry One and *Geometry Two* also have useful features that are not available in the *Geometric Supposers*:

- *Geometry One* offers opportunities for students to fully explore transformational and vector approaches to geometry in addition to traditional construction approaches. The *Supposers* only look at geometry through the CONSTRUCT mode and are limited to triangles, quadrilaterals, and circles.

- All three graphics modes are available to students simultaneously in *Geometry One* and *Two*. In the *Supposers*, different products must be used to work on triangles, quadrilaterals, and circles, respectively. In addition, students have more flexibility in the number and types of figures that can be on the screen at one time in *Geometry One*.

- *Geometry One* offers several special options that are not available in the *Supposers*. For example, it is possible to change the default length of drawn figures, to draw in three different colors, to change the line patterns, and to set up coordinate systems and reference frames of varying size and shape as a backdrop to figures drawn with the primary three modes.

- There is a well-developed course of instruction online in both *Geometry One* and *Geometry Two*. The *Supposers* are tools only with no specific format for presentation. (A substantial set of offline print materials has been developed to address this need in the *Supposers*. See Overview above.)

- *Geometry Two*, with its lessons and proof entry format, allows students to do traditional proofs online. No facility exists for doing proofs with the *Supposers*.

- In addition to a transformational graphics mode in *Geometry One*, there is also a proof sequence demonstrating how to do transformational proofs. This allows students to be exposed to and contrast varying axiomatic systems. ❑

Table of Comparative Features for *the Supposers* and *Geometry One/Two*

Feature	Availability in	
	Supposers	*Geometry 1/2*
Transformations		
Reflection	Limited	Yes
Translation	No	Yes
Rotation	No	Yes
Scale figures up or down	Limited	Yes
Shear	No	Yes
Pull (vertically or horizontally)	No	Yes
Vector Geometry		
Vector drawing	No	Yes
Mini-programming language	No	Yes
Special Graphics Features		
Auto. repeat ability for constructions	Yes	No
Coordinate systems & reference frames	No	Yes
Color capability	No	Yes
Fill capability (with color)	No	Yes
Erase option for drawings	Yes	Yes
Text ability on graphics screen	No	Yes
Useful for large screen demonstrations	Yes	Yes
Proofs		
Online proof entry	No	Yes
Ability to alter proof's graphic	No	Yes
Online proof checking capability	No	Yes
Instructional sequences		
Online activities which track student progress	No	Yes
Support print materials with tests	Yes	No
Constructions		
Points, lines, and line segments	Yes	Yes
Parallel and Perpendicular lines	Yes	Yes
Midpoints (midlines)	Yes	Yes
Rays	Yes	Yes
Arcs	No	Yes
Angles	Only Pre-supposer	Yes
Angle bisection	Yes	Cumbersome
Tangents	Yes	No
Circles	Yes	Yes
Automatic inscribed, circumscribed C's	Yes	No
Polygons	3- and 4-sided only	3–24 sides
Measurement		
Length, Angles	Yes	Yes
Area, Perimeter	Yes	No
Calculates comparison of two measures	Yes	No
Online data column	Yes	No

SPRING 1990

DIANNE F. KUSSATZ

Geometric Explorations

Exploring Geometry Using *GeoDraw*

The use of exploratory techniques can make the study of geometry, as well as all mathematics, tremendously exciting for both the teacher and the student. The tools available today via technology invite investigating geometry. Possibilities for allowing students to formulate and test their own conjectures are almost limitless.

IBM's *Geometry One* and *Geometry Two* include a tool, *GeoDraw*, which is conducive to exploring geometry as a laboratory course. *GeoDraw* has three interchangeable modes: CONSTRUCT, TRANSFORM, and V-DRAW, which allow one to create many difficult diagrams using only a few keystrokes. One example of the power of this tool is demonstrated in the following lab.

LABORATORY EXPERIMENT

OBJECTIVE:
The student will conduct several trials of the outlined experiment to discover that the ratio of the segments produced on each median of any triangle by their point of intersection is in a ratio of 2:1.

EXPERIMENT:
Perform several trials to investigate the relationship of the lengths of the medians and the segments on the medians of any triangle formed by their point of intersection. Include equilateral, isosceles, scalene, obtuse, and acute triangles. Formulate conjectures and arguments regarding the validity of your conjectures.

NOTE:
To repeat the measuring procedure on several triangles without having to construct a new triangle and its medians each time, we will construct one triangle with its medians and use PULL and SHEAR in TRANSFORM mode to "create" new trial triangles. Teachers may make directions as specific or general as desired.

The technique for using *GeoDraw* to complete this lab is described herein. First, select USE *GEODRAW* from the MAIN MENU. Use DELETE to erase a mistake. Be sure to hit ENTER as indicated. ❑

1. To **CONSTRUCT** AN EQUILATERAL TRIANGLE AND ITS MEDIANS, ENTER THE FOLLOWING:

KEY	RESPONSE TO INQUIRY ↓	COMMENTS
9		Enters construct mode.
N	3↵	Makes a regular *n*-gon with three sides.
4	C↵	Changes color to magenta.
M	AB↵	Constructs midpoints on the three
M	BC↵	sides of the triangle and labels them
		D, E, F.
M	AC↵	
S	AE↵	Constructs the three medians.
S	BF↵	
S	CD↵	
4	A↵	Changes the color back to black.
Alt + N*	AE CD↵↵	Labels intersection of medians with
		letter *G.*
F7 (function key)		Redraws any broken lines.

(*Alt prompts the use of the Alt key: + means the simultaneous use of keys.)

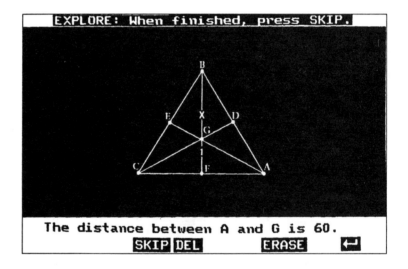

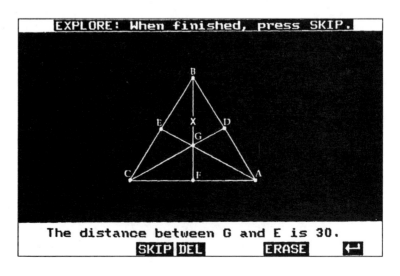

2. MEASURE THE MEDIANS AND EACH OF THEIR SEGMENTS.

KEY	RESPONSE TO INQUIRY	COMMENTS
—	↵↵	Enters measure mode.
D	AE↵↵	Measures distance from A to E.
D	AG↵↵	(Measure the appropriate segments
D	GE↵↵	and record the results on a lab sheet.)
D	BF↵↵	(There may be an error caused by
D	BG↵↵	rounding to the nearest pixel.)
D	GF↵↵	
D	CD↵↵	
D	CG↵↵	
D	GD↵↵	
F		Finish using the measure mode.

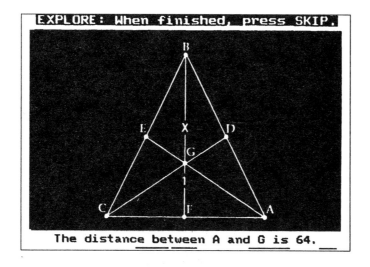

The distance between A and G is 64.

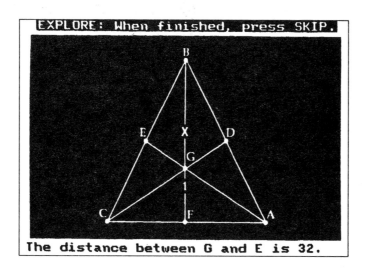

The distance between G and E is 32.

3. Investigate NEW triangles. To get new triangles, use the following procedure:

Key	Response to inquiry	Comments
0		Enters TRANSFORM mode.
D	ABCDEFG↵	Defines the figure to be transformed.
U	V 1.3↵	Pulls the figure vertically by a scale of 1.3 creating an isosceles triangle.

Repeat steps in #2 recording results on lab sheet.

Delete		Will erase the last construction and restore the original figure.
H	→→→↵	Shears to create an obtuse triangle.

Repeat steps in #2 recording results on lab sheet.

Delete		Erases the last figure.
H	←↵	Shears to create an acute triangle.

Repeat steps in #2 recording results on lab sheet.

Using PULL and SHEAR, create as many triangles as needed to complete the number of desired trials. Use the DELETE key to restore the figure to its original form.

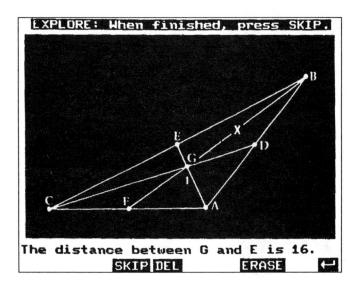

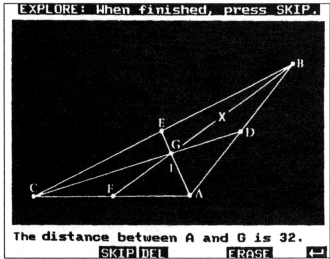

4. Formulate conjectures and verify.

Techniques such as the one described above keep the tedious constructions to a minimum allowing for concentration on the concepts being investigated.

WINTER 1991

JONATHAN CHOATE

Sketchpad Modeling

Recently, a powerful new geometric program was introduced that could have a significant impact on both the teaching and learning of geometry, and in solving problems like the art gallery and ice hockey problems [in past issues of *Consortium*]. The program, called the *Geometer's Sketchpad*, is currently available only for Macintosh computers, but I wouldn't be surprised if it was available for IBM-compatible machines in the not-too-distant future. Sketchpad takes full advantage of a windows-oriented environment; it is a visually appealing and user-friendly program. **FIGURE 1** shows a typical screen.

The tool palette on the left contains tools for constructing points, circles, lines, line-segments, rays, and for labeling a figure. Points, lines, and circles are constructed by highlighting the appropriate tool with the

mouse, clicking on the screen, and then dragging with the mouse until the desired object appears on the screen. This is an object-oriented program where to do anything, you must first click on the object(s) you want to do something to, and then click on the desired operation from the menus at the top of the screen. For example,

- to construct the midpoint of a previously drawn segment, first highlight the segment, then pull down the CONSTRUCT menu and click on MIDPOINT OF LINE.
- to measure, $\angle ABC$, highlight points A, B, and C, in that order, and click on ANGLE from the MEASURE menu.
- to construct a perpendicular to a line through a point not on a line, highlight the point and the line, then click on PERPENDICULAR LINE from the CONSTRUCT menu.

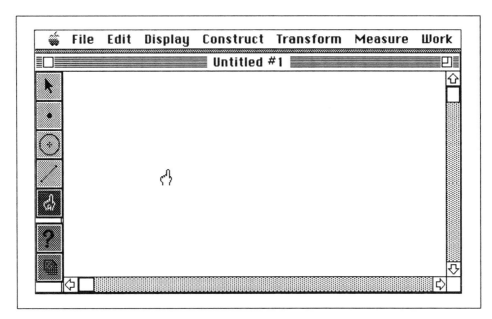

FIGURE 1. THE *GEOMETER'S SKETCHPAD* SCREEN AS IT APPEARS ON THE COMPUTER.

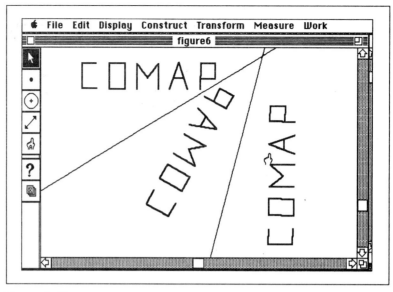

FIGURE 2. TRANSFORMING AN OBJECT ON THE SCREEN.

- to construct the segment between two points, highlight the two points, then click on SEGMENT from the CONSTRUCT menu.

Objects on the screen are transformed in a similar way. In **Figure 2**, the reflected image of the word "COMAP," was constructed as follows: line *l* was highlighted and selected as an axis of reflection using the TRANSFORM menu; "COMAP" was highlighted and REFLECT was selected from the TRANSFORM menu. The reflected image was then reflected in line *p*. All the preceding figures can be constructed using existing software such as *Geometric Supposer* and *Geometry Grapher*.

There are, however, some things that the *Sketchpad* can do that others cannot and that transform the *Sketchpad* into a powerful modeling tool. First of all, you can use it to construct dynamic demonstrations of geometric theorems. Here are some examples:

1. Consider ΔABC constructed in **Figure 3**. The measurements of the six parts are listed below the figure. To change this image, all you need to do is take the mouse, click on one of the vertices, say A, and holding the button down, drag A to another part of the screen. The whole diagram changes as A is moved to its

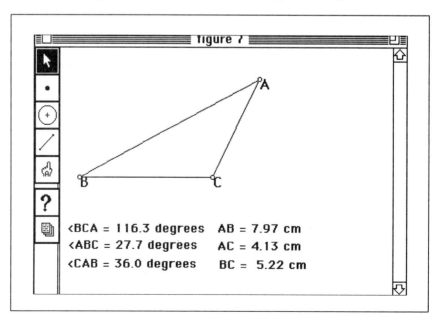

FIGURE 3.

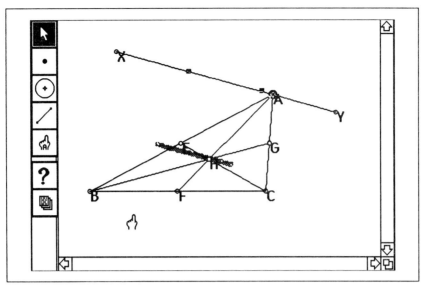

FIGURE 4.

new location. All the measurements are also updated. The measurements also demonstrate that the sum of the angles of a triangle is equal to 180°.

2. In addition, one can trace the movement of other points in a triangle. In **Figure 4**, $\triangle ABC$ has been constructed along with its "centroid" G. (A *centroid* is the point of intersection of the lines joining the three vertices to the midpoints of their respective opposite sides.) *Sketchpad* allows you to move A and trace the path of the centroid. To do this, all you need do is highlight point G and then click on TRACE POINT from the DISPLAY menu. Every time you move a vertex of the triangle with the mouse, the path of the centroid will be traced. *Sketchpad* also has a feature called ANIMATE that allows you to construct a point on a circle or line segment and then make the point move back and forth on the segment, or go around and around at a constant speed.

Solutions to the following problem posed by Jim Wilson, head of the Mathematics Education Department at the University of Georgia, can be found using this feature.

PROBLEM

1. Construct a triangle, $\triangle ABC$, and a line segment XY that contains A.
2. Construct the centroid G and the orthocenter H of $\triangle ABC$.
3. What curve does the centroid trace out as point A moves back and forth on segment XY?
4. What curve does the orthocenter trace out?

Figure 4, produced by *Sketchpad*, suggests that the answer to the first part of this question is a line segment parallel to XY.

3. TRACE and ANIMATE can also be used to construct a hyperbola in the following way.

1. Construct a line segment AB.
2. Construct the midpoint C of AB.
3. Construct the perpendicular bisector of AB.
4. Construct points D and E on the perpendicular bisector such that D is above AB and E is below AB. Construct segment DE.
5. Let F be any point on DE and construct the circle with center F and radius equal to AF.

6. Construct a line through *F* parallel to *AB*.

7. Construct the intersections *G* and *H* of the line constructed in Step 6 with the circle constructed in Step 5.

Points *G* and *H* both lie on a hyperbola, which can now be drawn by putting a TRACE on points *G* and *H* and then animating point *F* on line segment *DE*. **Figure 5** shows the result.

Another feature that is very useful is the SCRIPT feature. This allows you to save a construction, once you have made it, as a macro and use it again in future constructions. For example, given a line segment *AB*, one can construct on *AB* an equilateral triangle with *AB* as one of the sides. This can be saved and used later on whenever one needs an equilateral triangle with sides equal in length to a given segment. Similarly, one could develop a construction that trisects a line segment. This would allow students to build collections of scripts, which could be used as tools in later work. Scripts are saved as a list of the steps used in the construction written out in clear, precise English.

What makes the *Sketchpad* unique is that it allows you to play with geometric objects and analyze what happens in ways never before possible. It allows you to build geometric models and to learn from them. It allows students to put to use the advice given by Richard Feynmann, the Nobel laureate physicist, to his student at Cal. Tech. Carter Mead (one of the inventors of the silicone chips used in microcomputers) about how to solve problems.

"…Learn to listen to what the problem is trying to tell you. Don't tell it all the math you already know."

In other words, play with the problem until it tells you something useful. This, in the long run, may be the most important feature of *Sketchpad*: the program's ability to build dynamic models of problems such as the art gallery problem, which allow us to "hear" what a problem is trying to tell us. ❑

REFERENCES

Geometer's Sketchpad. Berkeley: Key Curriculum Press.

Geometric Supposer Series. Pleasantville, NY: Sunburst Publications.

Geometry Grapher. Boston: Houghton Mifflin Co.

Gilder, L. 1990. *Microcosm.* New York: Basic Books.

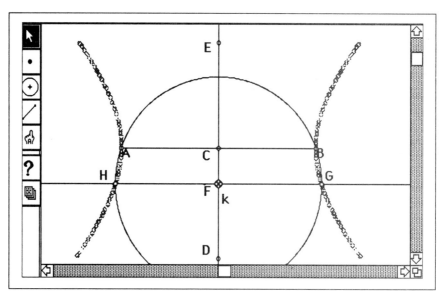

FIGURE 5.

Spring 1993

JONATHAN CHOATE

Fractal Magic for Spring

Editor's Note: *This semester I am teaching a fractal geometry elective. The following article was a collaborative effort with four of my students: Jason Mather, Gautam Sardesai, Katie Wallace, and Nils van Otterloo, who produced all the illustrations for this article.*

In previous [articles, we have shown] that coastlines have a peculiar geometry. [We have seen] that measuring a coastline was no easy task because as one uses a shorter and shorter unit, the perimeter of the coastline grows and grows. This phenomenon was first studied by Lewis Richardson in 1961 and it was this property of coastlines and other natural forms which led Benoit Mandelbrot to the discovery of what is now called fractal geometry. In his book, *The Fractal Geometry of Nature*, Mandelbrot created a variety of mathematical models for natural forms that have this interesting yet perplexing property: they are bounded yet have an infinite perimeter. Since none of the algebraic curves studied in the secondary curriculum have this property, we cannot give an equation in the classical sense for these curves, so we have to find another way to generate them. Here is how Mandelbrot generated curves that describe natural forms such as coastlines and plants.

The limiting shape of the process defined in **Figure 1**, the Koch snowflake curve, is a good model for coastlines and is an example of a fractal. Notice that in this example, each successive pre-fractal is four-thirds longer than the preceding one and hence the snowflake curve must have an infinite perimeter. Notice also that each succeeding

pre-fractal consists of copies of the preceding level pre-fractal. Thus, fractals are geometric objects that consist of an infinite number of copies of themselves. This infinite self-similarity is one of the fascinating aspects of fractals. By changing the generator, one can get very different-looking coastline curves varying from very smooth ones, good for modeling tropical coastlines, to very jagged ones, appropriate for modeling a very rough coastline like that of Norway.

HOW TO GET A COMPUTER TO GENERATE A COASTLINE CURVE

The preceding defines fractals recursively and can be used to generate fractal images on a computer. Przemyslaw Prusinkiewicz, a computer scientist, and Aristid Lindenmayer, a theoretical biologist, developed a variation of this method to model other natural forms such as plants, bushes, and trees. Their method, often referred to as *L-strings* (named for Lindenmayer), can be used to generate a Koch curve. Here's how.

1. Start with an *axiom*

    F

    where F means "move forward." This defines L_0, the initiator.

FIGURE 1.

How to Generate a
Coastline Curve: GENERATING THE KOCH

SNOWFLAKE CURVE AND ITS PARTS,

WHICH MODEL A COASTLINE.

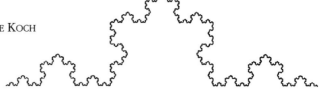

STEP 0: START WITH A LINE SEGMENT L_0. THIS IS CALLED THE *INITIATOR*. ASSUME THAT L_0 HAS LENGTH 1.

L_0

STEP 1: CREATE A NEW SHAPE L_1, WHICH CONSISTS OF SCALED-DOWN COPIES OF L_0 THAT HAVE LENGTH 1/3. THIS IS CALLED THE *GENERATOR* AND HAS LENGTH 4/3. SINCE THE SEGMENTS MAKING UP THE GENERATOR ARE ONE-THIRD THE LENGTH OF THE INITIATOR, 1/3 IS CALLED THE *SCALE FACTOR*. L_1 IS CALLED A *LEVEL-1 PRE-FRACTAL*.

L_1

STEP 2: CREATE A NEW SHAPE L_2 BY REPLACING EVERY SEGMENT IN L_1 WITH SCALED-DOWN COPIES OF THE GENERATOR, WHICH HAVE BEEN SCALED DOWN BY A FACTOR OF 1/3. SINCE L_2 CONSISTS OF FOUR COPIES OF L_1 EACH OF LENGTH 4/9, IT HAS A PERIMETER OF 16/9.

L_2

STEP 3: CREATE A NEW SHAPE L_3 BY REPLACING EVERY SEGMENT IN L_2 WITH SCALED-DOWN COPIES OF THE GENERATOR, WHICH HAVE BEEN SCALED DOWN BY A FACTOR OF 1/3. SINCE L_3 CONSISTS OF FOUR COPIES OF L_2 EACH OF LENGTH 16/27, IT HAS A PERIMETER OF 64/27. EVENTUALLY, YOU WILL REACH A LEVEL K SUCH THAT THE

L_3

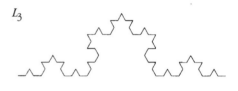

L_4

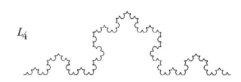

LENGTH OF A SEGMENT IS LESS THAN ONE PIXEL AND IT IS TIME TO STOP.

STEP K + 1: CREATE A NEW SHAPE L_{K+1} BY REPLACING EVERY SEGMENT IN L_K WITH SCALED-DOWN COPIES OF THE GENERATOR, WHICH HAVE BEEN SCALED DOWN BY A FACTOR OF $(1/3)^{K-1}$.

2. Give a *production rule*

$$F \rightarrow F + F - - F + F$$

where + means "turn counter-clockwise 60 degrees" and – means "turn clockwise 60 degrees." With the preceding in mind, the string $F + F - - F + F$ can be interpreted as meaning

- F, go forward
- +, turn counter-clockwise 60°
- F, go forward
- –, turn clockwise 60°
- –, turn clockwise 60°
- F, go forward
- +, turn counter-clockwise 60°
- F, go forward.

The Koch snowflake method works fine for coastlines, but not so well for trees and bushes and other forms that have branches. To create forms that have branches, we need two more L-string commands: "[" and "]" where [means "store the current position and heading," and] means "return to where you were when [was encountered." If the turn angle designated by +/– is 30°, then the string F [+ F] F [– F] F means

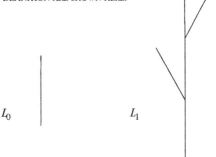

FIGURE 2.
HOW TO GENERATE A BUSH
WITH SEGMENT REWRITING

FRACTAL BUSH CREATED BY USING L-STRINGS WITH [AND] AND THE PRODUCTION RULE

$$F \rightarrow F [+ F] F [– F] F.$$

LEVELS 0, 1, 2, 3, AND 6 PRE-FRACTALS PRODUCED USING THIS DEFINITION ARE SHOWN HERE.

- F, GO FORWARD
- [, SAVE YOUR CURRENT LOCATION X AND CURRENT HEADING H
- +, TURN COUNTER-CLOCKWISE 60°
- F, GO FORWARD
-], RETURN TO X AND RESET YOUR HEADING TO H
- F, GO FORWARD
- [, SAVE YOUR CURRENT LOCATION X AND CURRENT HEADING H
- –, TURN CLOCKWISE 60°
- F, GO FORWARD,
-], RETURN TO X AND RESET YOUR HEADING TO H,
- F, GO FORWARD

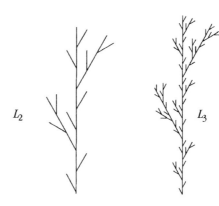

The string F + F – – F + F can be thought of as a set of directions for traversing the generator, L_1, for a Koch curve. Those of you who know LOGO should recognize F + F – – F + F as a turtle graphics description of L_1. F → F + F – – F + F is called a *production rule* because, to get the directions for traversing the level-2 Koch curve, all you have to do is replace every F in the level-1 string with F + F – – F + F. Thus, the level-2 Koch curve is defined by

F + F – – F + F + F + F – – F
+ F – – F + F – – F
+ F + F + F – – F + F.

To get the level-3 pre-fractal, replace every F in the level-2 string with F + F – – F + F. Using this method, you can produce the string and hence turtle graphics instructions for any level pre-fractal desired.

Since most computer languages have extensive string manipulation capabilities, it is easy to get a computer to generate the string for whatever level desired. It may take some time, but it can be done. If the language also has graphics capabilities, routines can be written which can be used to translate the L-string into a sequence of commands that will draw the pre-fractal. For more on implementing L-strings on a computer see Burns's "The Flowering of String Rewriting Systems," or write to me and I will send you some annotated BASIC subroutines that will do the job.

Writing a program to generate fractal images using this method is a good computer science project and could be done by anyone in a beginning programming course who has had some trigonometry. Notice that no mention is made of the scaling factor used by Mandelbrot in this method. This is taken care of in the program by calculating a scaling factor such that each new pre-fractal fits in the same size viewing rectangle that the preceding one did.

All the L-string figures shown in **Figure 2** use a technique that Prusinkiewicz and Lindenmayer refer to as *segment rewriting*. This means that to get the next level pre-fractal, all the segments of the current level are replaced by scaled-down copies of the generator. This works well for very bushy structures but not for natural forms that have trunks and long branches. To model these, Prusinkiewicz and Lindenmayer use a technique called *node rewriting*. Nodes are points where there are branches and usually occur in L-strings between [and]. Node rewriting means placing at each node a scaled-down copy of the generator. In **Figure 3**, an example of node rewriting is shown.

Once you get the hang of it, you will find that L-strings are easy to define and use and that you can create very realistic computer-generated natural forms. In a future Modeler's Corner, I will show another much faster way to generate natural forms, because, as you will find out, the higher the level pre-fractal, the longer it takes to generate it. I will also show how you can model more complex natural forms such as flowers. If any of you generate some forms of your own, send them to me and I'll include them in a future column. ❑

FIGURE 3.
HOW TO GENERATE A BUSH
WITH NODE REWRITING

FRACTAL BUSH CREATED BY USING NODE REWRITING.

HERE IS HOW NODE REWRITING WAS USED TO CREATE THIS BUSH.

1. START WITH AN AXIOM

X

WHERE X IS A DUMMY WORD WHOSE TURTLE GRAPHIC MEANING IS "DO NOTHING."

2. GIVE TWO PRODUCTION RULES

$$X \rightarrow F [+ X] F [- X] + X$$
$$F \rightarrow FF$$

AND LET THE TURN ANGLE BE $30°$.

THE PRECEDING DEFINES THE FOLLOWING SEQUENCES OF COMMANDS FOR GENERATING THE PRE-FRACTALS.

LEVEL 0: X , DO NOTHING

LEVEL 1: F [+ X] F [– X] + X, WHICH SIMPLIFIES TO FF SINCE X INTERPRETED AS A TURTLE GRAPHICS COMMAND MEANS DO NOTHING. THIS DRAWS A STRAIGHT LINE WITH TWO NODES. AT THE FIRST ONE, THERE WILL BE ONE BRANCH AND AT THE SECOND TWO BRANCHES.

LEVEL 2: FF [+ F [+ X] F [–X] + X] FF [– F [+ X] F [–X] + X] + F [+ X] F [–X] + X, WHICH SIMPLIFIES TO FF [+ FF] FF [– FF] + FF. THIS DEFINES THE GENERATOR THAT WILL BE REPEATED AT ALL FUTURE NODES.

LEVEL 3: FIRST REPLACE EACH F IN THE DEFINING STRING FOR LEVEL 2 WITH FF.

FFFF [+ FF [+ X] FF [– X] + X] FFFF [– FF [+ X] FF [– X] + X] + FF [+ X] FF [– X] + X

NEXT, REPLACE EACH X WITH F [+ X] F [– X] + X.

FFFF [+ FF [+ F [+ X] F [–X] + X] FF [– F [+ X] F [–X] + X] + F [+ X] F [–X] + X] FFFF [– FF [+ F [+ X] F [–X] + X] FF [– F [+ X] F [–X] + X] + F [+ X] F [–X] + X] + FF [+ F [+ X] F [–X] + X] FF [– F [+ X] F [–X] + X] + X

DELETING EACH X, ONE GETS
FFFF [+ FF [+ FF] FF [– FF] + FF] FFFF [– FF [+ FF] FF [– FF] + FF] + FF [+ FF] FF [– FF] + FF,

WHICH IS THE TURTLE GRAPHIC DESCRIPTION OF THE LEVEL-3 PRE–FRACTAL CONTAINING THREE COPIES OF THE GENERATOR.

L_6

L_3

L_1

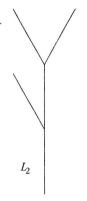

L_2

L_4

SOME NOTES ON SOFTWARE

The fractals in this article were produced by Jason, Gautam, Katie and Nils using the software described below.

- To generate images using Mandelbrot's Initiator/Generator definition, we used *Fract-o-Graph* and *Designer Fractal*. Both are Macintosh programs which make use of the mouse to define the generators. *Fract-o-Graph* is very easy to use and is appropriate for younger students. *Designer Fractal* is a bit harder to use but offers a variety of options for generating more complicated types of fractals.For those of you who would like to work through Mandelbrot's *Fractal Geometry of Nature*, this would be an ideal piece of software.

- To generate images using L-strings, we used *Fractal Factory* and *L-Strings*. *Fractal Factory* is available only for the IBM. It was designed for use in a high school geometry course and comes with a geometric construction program called *Geometry Grapher*. It is very easy to use and comes with a tutorial, which contains a mini-course on L-strings but does not allow the use of [and]. *L-Strings* is a comprehensive, easy-to-use Macintosh program that permits all L-string commands, many of which are not mentioned in this article.

REFERENCES

Barnsley, Michael. 1988. *Fractals Everywhere*. San Diego: Academic Press.

Burns, Anne M. 1992. The flowering of string rewriting systems. *The College Mathematics Journal* 23(3): 225–236.

Garcia, Linda. 1991. *The Fractal Explorer*. Media Magic, P.O. Box 598, Nicasio, CA 94946

Mandelbrot, Benoit. 1982. *The Fractal Geometry of Nature*. San Francisco: W.H. Freeman.

McGuire, Michael. 1991. *An Eye For Fractals*. Reading, MA: Addison-Wesley.

Prusinkiewicz, Przemyslaw and Aristid Lindenmayer. 1990. *The Algorithmic Beauty of Plants*. New York: Springer-Verlag.

Heinz-Otto Peitgen, Dietmar Saupe, eds. 1988. *The Science of Fractal Images*. New York: Springer-Verlag.

SOFTWARE

Bourke, Paul. *L-Strings*, Macintosh. Media Magic, P.O. Box 598, Nicasio, CA, 94946.

Caswell, Dennis. *FractoGraph*, Macintosh. Send 3.5" disk and self-addressed mailer to Jonathan Choate, Groton School, Groton, MA, 01450.

Choate, Jonathan. *Geometry Grapher and Fractal Factory*, IBM. Boston: Houghton Mifflin.

Dynamic Software. *Designer Fractal*, Macintosh. Media Magic, P.O. Box 598, Nicasio, CA, 94946.

Section 3

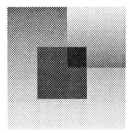

The articles in this section show why the graphing calculator has become so popular so quickly. The already powerful features of these devices can be enhanced with programs. Indeed, programming these calculators is so commonplace that newer models now on the market allow the exchange of programs between similar machines.

Although these programs were written for the TI–81 and Casio graphing calculators, they can be adapted to other graphing calculators currently available.

SPRING 1991

GARY FROELICH

Iteration

Consider a simple system of equations: $y = x - 6$, $y = 8 - 2x$. It follows that $x - 6 = 8 - 2x$ and $x = 14 - 2x$. Mathematics teachers often cringe when students express a variable as a function of itself. Through the process of iteration, however, this form can often be made useful.

Begin by picking any value for x, say 1. Then $14 - 2(1) = 12$. Because $x = 14 - 2x$, the value of $14 - 2x$ is also a value of x. One then has $14 - 2(12) = -10$. Similarly, $14 - 2(-10) = 34$. This process may be continued indefinitely and is called *iteration*.

The Curriculum and Evaluation Standards of the National Council of Teachers of Mathematics places great emphasis on the development of a "core curriculum." The authors of the *Standards* believe that many topics in secondary mathematics can be studied by all students. Students of differing abilities, however, are seen as approaching a particular topic in different ways.

An important assumption is that students will learn new approaches to problems as their mathematical sophistication grows. Technology has provided secondary students with dramatic new approaches to solving problems. This column considers *iteration*, a useful problem-solving tool that has been made more practical by the availability of inexpensive computer software and scientific calculators. Iteration can sometimes produce solutions where algebraic and computer graphing methods fail.

Of what use is iteration? One can see that, in the example given, continuation of the process results in values that grow without limit. Consider $x = 14 - 2x$ again. It follows that $2x = 14 - x$ and $x = (14 - x)/2$. Starting with $x = 1$ results in $(14 - 1)/2 = 6.5$. The new value of x gives $(14 - 6.5)/2 = 3.75$, which gives $(14 - 3.75)/2 = 5.125$. Repeated applications approximate 4-2/3, the solution for x in the original system.

Iteration, of course, is a computationally intense process, but technology provides a number of tools that make it a very practical problem-solving method. Considered next are three such tools: computer spreadsheets, graphing utilities, and calculators.

A simple, two-column spreadsheet model for the iterative process can be constructed in minutes. To model the previous example, place a 1 in cell A1 of the spreadsheet. Place the formula $(14 - A1)/2$ in cell B1. In cell A2, place the formula B1. Then, copy the formula in cell B1 into cell B2. The spreadsheet will automatically change the A1 in the formula to A2. Now, copy row 2 of the spreadsheet into the next several rows. A table similar to the following will be produced.

1.00	6.50
6.50	3.75
3.75	5.13
5.13	4.44
4.44	4.78
4.78	4.61
4.61	4.70
4.70	4.65
4.65	4.67

Calculators such as the graphing models from Casio and Texas Instruments feature an ANSWER key that simplifies iteration. On the TI–81, for example, the previous result can be obtained by typing a 1 and pressing ENTER, then typing $(14 - \text{ANS})/2$ and pressing ENTER again. The remaining values in the second column of the spreadsheet model are obtained by repeatedly pressing the ENTER key.

Many students find a geometric model of the iterative process helpful. One can be obtained by graphing $y = x$, and $y = (14 - x)/2$. The initial value, $x = 1$, is plotted on the x-axis and connected to the point $(1, 6.5)$ on $y = (14 - x)/2$.

Because the y-value of 6.5 becomes the new x-value, this point is connected to $(6.5, 6.5)$ on $y = x$, which is connected to $(6.5, 3.75)$ on $y = (14 - x)/2$. The continuation of the process results in a nice geometric demonstration of the convergence toward the x-value in the solution of the original system.

The result is shown in **Figure 1**. The divergence seen in the previous attempt to

iterate $x = 14 - 2x$ is depicted in **Figure 2**. A geometric demonstration of iteration is possible with almost any graphing device that plots points and draws segments. A program that produces such a demonstration on the TI–81 is listed here.

```
Prgm2:ITERATE
ClrDraw
Input A
DispGraph
Line (Xmin, Xmin, Xmax, Xmax)
A -> X
Line (X, O, X, Y1)
Pause
Lbl A
Line (X, Y1, Y1, Y1)
Pause
Y1 -> X
Line (X, X, X, Y1)
Pause
Goto A
End
```

The function to iterate is typed as Y1 using the Y= key. The range is set using the RANGE screen. The program prompts the user for the initial value of x and pauses after each segment is drawn. The user must press ENTER in order to see the next segment. Touching the calculator's ON key will cause to program to terminate.

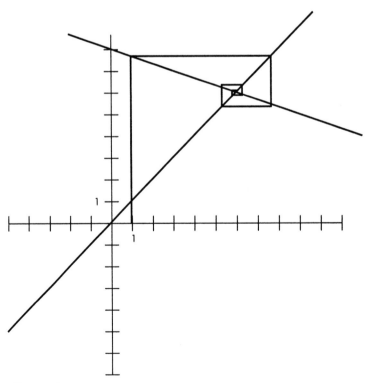

FIGURE 1.

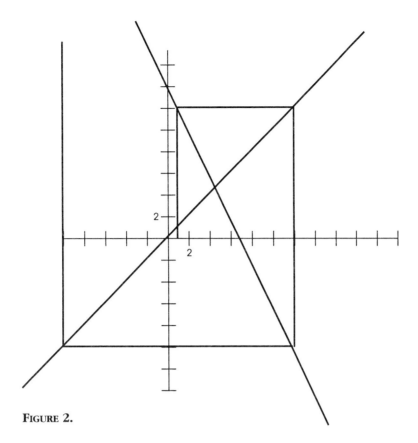

FIGURE 2.

Some computer mathematics utilities provide an iteration feature. The ITERATES function of version 2.0 of *Derive*, for example, returns successive iterations when the user supplies the function, the initial value, and the number of iterations. (See **Figure 3**.)

Iteration requires that a variable be expressed in terms of itself. Sometimes the resulting iteration diverges, sometimes it converges. As students become familiar with the process as a problem-solving tool, they develop a feel for which iteration will diverge, and which iteration will converge.

Consider, for example, the quadratic equation $x^2 - x - 12 = 0$. Solving for the x in the linear term gives $x = x^2 - 12$. Repeated iteration is likely to give a divergent result because repeated squaring causes rapid growth. Is the same true if an initial value smaller than 1 is used?

```
1: ITERATES

2: [1, 6.5, 3.75, 5.125, 4.4375, 4.78125, 4.60937, 4.69531, 4.65234, 4.67382]

COMMAND: Author Build Calculus Declare Expand Factor Help Jump soLve Manage
              Options Plot Quit Remove Simplify Transfer moVe Window approX
Compute Time: 0.3 seconds
Simp (1)                        Free: 100%            Derive Algebra
```

FIGURE 3.

Solving for the x in the quadratic term gives $x = \sqrt{(x+12)}$. Repeated applications of the square root do not result in unlimited growth. One of the solutions is achieved by iteration of this function. The results are shown in the spreadsheet below.

1.00	3.61
3.61	3.95
3.95	3.99
3.99	4.00
4.00	4.00

How does one obtain the second solution? Reflect $x^2 - x - 12$ through the y-axis:

$$(-x)^2 - (-x) - 12 = x^2 + x - 12.$$

Solve $x^2 + x - 12 = 0$ for x to obtain $x = \sqrt{(12 - x)}$. Choose an initial value smaller than 12 and iterate. The results are shown in the spreadsheet below.

1.00	3.32
3.32	2.95
2.95	3.01
3.01	3.00
3.00	3.00

Because of the reflection through the y-axis, the actual solution is −3 rather than 3.

The results of iteration can depend on the initial value chosen, and convergence and divergence are not the only types of behavior exhibited. The reader is invited, for example, to use a spreadsheet, graphing utility, or calculator to explore the behavior that occurs when iterating $x = 0.3(x - 3)^2 + 8$.

The power of iteration is more dramatic when one is faced with an equation that defies other methods. A cubic polynomial with three irrational zeros, for example, is difficult to solve algebraically, although the zeros are easily approximated with a graphing utility. Graphing utilities can fail where iteration succeeds, however. The equation $2x = x^{10}$ presents problems for many graphing utilities (see Idea Exchange, *Consortium* 27). All three solutions can be obtained by iteration. The reader is invited to attempt them. ❏

GARY FROELICH

The Victory Arc

The *Curriculum and Evaluations Standards* of the National Council of Teachers of Mathematics place strong emphasis on technology and mathematical modeling. This article considers an example of modeling made accessible by technology that is suitable for secondary students familiar with quadratic functions and systems of equations. An extension for trigonometry students is also discussed. In an article in the February 4, 1991, issue of *U.S. News & World Report*, Stephen Budiansky, Bruce Auster, and Peter Cary report on what was then the possible ground war in the Persian Gulf. Among the weaponry discussed is the firefinder radar used by U.S. forces to track enemy artillery shells. A graphic in the article depicts the radar's plotting of a parabolic arc to locate a shell's origin.

An investigation of the mathematics behind this technology is possible for secondary students who have access to a graphing utility such as the TI–81 graphing calculator or a computer graphing utility such as the IBM *Mathematics Exploration Toolkit* (MET).

Students should be aware that an object thrown or fired upward follows a parabolic path. They should also be familiar with the general quadratic equation for a parabola, $f(x) = ax^2 + bx + c$, and should be able to solve a 3 X 3 system of equations, preferably using matrices.

To demonstrate the detection of an artillery launch, enter and run the following TI–81 program.

```
Prgm4:LAUNCH
0→Xmin
500→Xmax
0→Ymin
100→Ymax
PT–On(300, 21)
Pause
Pt–On(250, 29.75)
Pause
Pt–On(200, 26)
Pause
Input
End
```

The program places a dot on the graphics screen to simulate the appearance on a radar screen of a point in the trajectory of the shell. Pressing the ENTER key causes a second dot to appear, and pressing it again causes a third dot to appear (**Figure 1**). Pressing ENTER a third time places a moveable cursor on the screen so that the coordinates of the three points may be read.

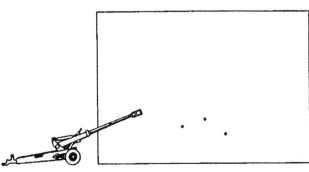

FIGURE 1.

Suppose that the coordinates are (200, 25.4), (252.63, 30.16), and (300, 20.63). To find the equation of the parabolic arc, solve the system

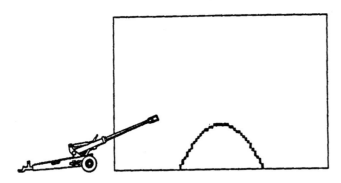

FIGURE 2.

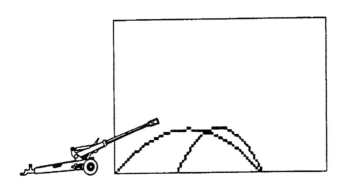

FIGURE 3.

$$25.4 = 200^2a + 200b + c,$$
$$30.16 = 252.63^2a + 252.63b + c,$$
$$20.63 = 300^2a + 300b + c.$$

The system is quickly solved by finding the product of the inverse of the matrix of coefficients and the column matrix of constants.

$$\begin{bmatrix} 40,000 & 200 & 1 \\ 63,821.92 & 252.63 & 1 \\ 90,000 & 300 & 1 \end{bmatrix}^{-1} \begin{bmatrix} 25.4 \\ 30.16 \\ 20.63 \end{bmatrix} = \begin{bmatrix} -0.00292 \\ 1.41043 \\ -140.04 \end{bmatrix}$$

Enter the first matrix on the TI–81 as matrix A and the second as matrix B, then type $[A]^{-1}$ * $[B]$ to solve the system.

Plot the shell's trajectory by graphing $y = -0.00292x^2 + 1.41043x - 140.04$ (**Figure 2**). Trace the curve and verify that it approximates the trajectory by observing the coordinate readout.

Continue tracing to the parabola's right-most intercept to locate the source of the artillery fire about 343 units to the right of the coordinate system's origin. Or, alternately, use the quadratic formula to find the zeros of the function. Pinpointing the location of the launch, of course, enables retaliation and students are impressed by a demonstration. Suppose your location is at the origin of the coordinate system and that the function $f(x) = -0.001x(x - E)$, where E represents the distance to the enemy artillery, governs the operation of your artillery. Plot this function with $E = 343$ to simulate the return fire (**Figure 3**).

Enter this function on the TI–81 as Y2 and leave the model of the enemy artillery fire as Y1. Press GRAPH and the calculator first plots the trajectory of the enemy fire and then plots the return fire. According to *U.S. News & World Report*, the return fire is often launched before the enemy fire hits the ground!

A more realistic model of fire-return fire is possible if students are familiar with trigonometry and parametric plotting. If an object at the origin of the coordinate system is thrown upward with an initial velocity of v feet per second at an angle of α degrees, then a parametric model for its location after t seconds is $x = vt \cos \alpha$, $y = vt \sin \alpha - 16t^2$ [Demana and Waits 1990].

Calculation of the parabolic arc and the location of the enemy artillery are the same as in the previous model. The calculation of return fire, however, is done differently.

Assuming that the return fire is launched with equipment that fires at a fixed velocity, the problem is to determine the angle at which return fire should be launched in order to hit the enemy's location.

1 To pinpoint enemy artillery batteries, U.S. forces use an automated radar system that tracks incoming shells. Radar scans across a 90° arc, searching for hostile fire.

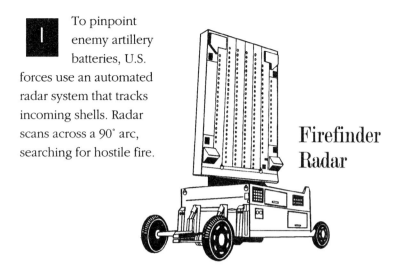

Firefinder Radar

2 When a shell is detected, radar tracks its trajectory in three dimensions.

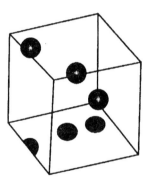

3 Computer plots a parabolic arc through the flight path to calculate point of origin.

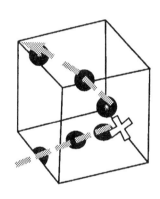

4 Coordinates are automatically transmitted to artillery fire control computer, which elevates and traverses gun.

Incoming shell

5 Seconds after an enemy battery fires, return fire has begun—even before the incoming round has landed.

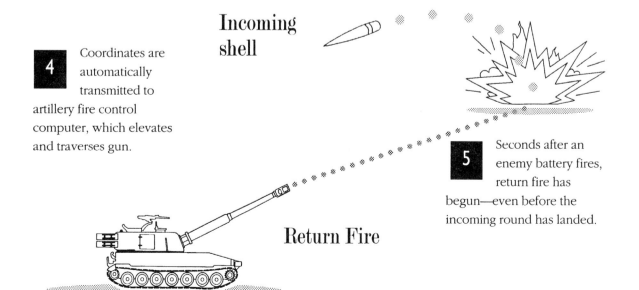

Return Fire

Solve the two parametric equations described above for t, set them equal to each other, and place the resulting quadratic in general form to obtain these transformations: $a = -16/(v \cos \alpha)^2$, $b = \tan \alpha$, $c = 0$, $\alpha = \tan^{-1} b$, and $v = \sqrt{((-16(b^2 + 1)/a)}$.

Substitute for a, b, and c in $y = ax^2 + bx + c$, and factor to get $y = -16/(v \cos \alpha)^2 x (x - \sin (2\alpha)v^2/32)$. Thus E, the enemy location in the first model, is equal to $\sin (2\alpha)v^2/32$. Assume a fixed return fire velocity of 150 feet per second and solve $\sin(2\alpha)150^2/32 = 343$ for α to obtain 14.60°, the correct angle at which to elevate artillery for return fire.

The TI–81 allows plotting of the parametric model by changing the calculator's graphing mode from FUNCTION to PARAMETRIC. The PARAMETRIC mode's range screen includes settings for t. A T_{min} of 0 and a T_{max} of 5 in steps of 0.1 are reasonable for this model, but a precise calculation of the time required for a projectile to complete its path can be made by evaluating $v \sin(\alpha)/16$, one of the zeros of $y = vt \sin \alpha - 16t^2$, for $v = 150$ and $\alpha = 14.60°$.

The trajectory of the enemy projectile can be modeled in more than one way. Enter the parametric equations $x = t$, $y = -0.00292t^2 + 1.41043t - 140.04$ and plot. Try reversing the values of T_{min} and T_{max} and using a negative T_{step}. Note that in this case, t does not represent time.

An alternate method is to choose a velocity (v) and angle of elevation (α), and plot the parametric equations $x = vt \cos \alpha + 343$, $y = vt \sin \alpha - 16t^2$ with $90° \leq \alpha \leq 180°$.

The actual distances and velocities on the battlefield are many times those used in the models given here. According to *U.S. News & World Report*, the best artillery has a range near 20 miles. ❑

REFERENCES

Budiansky, Stephen with Bruce B. Auster and Peter Cary. 1991. The Gulf War: Preparing the Ground. *U.S. News & World Report.* (February 4, 1991): 32–41.

Demana, Franklin, and Bert K. Waits. 1990. *Precalculus Mathematics: A Graphing Approach.* Reading, MA: Addison-Wesley.

SPRING 1992

GARY FROELICH

Actual Value vs. Predicted Value

Developing a Residual Plot Program with the TI–81 Calculator

Current efforts in reform of the school mathematics curriculum place strong emphasis on data analysis. Introductory experiences suitable for middle school students include construction of scatter plots and fitting lines to data. (See Froelich, Bartkovich and Foerster [1991] and Landwehr and Watkins [1986].) Advanced techniques include fitting exponential, logarithmic, polynomial and trigonometric functions to data. (See Foerster [1987], Moore and McCabe [1989], and North Carolina School of Science and Mathematics [1991].)

Common to all these topics is the emphasis they place on mathematical modeling. There is little doubt that students who study data analysis have a heightened appreciation of the role mathematics plays in the world around them.

Mathematical models are seldom perfect, and the imperfections are of great concern to those who develop models. The amount by which a model misses the correct prediction when it is applied to data used to generate the model is known as a *residual*. If, for example, a function used to model the relationship between the time that a liquid has been flowing from a container and the amount of liquid remaining predicts that there are 3 liters remaining after 10 seconds, but there were actually 2.5 liters remaining, then the residual is 0.5 liters.

Actually, the residual in the previous example is –0.5 liters. Although it is best not to consider sign when working with beginning students, the correct definition of residual is the actual value minus the predicted value.

Of course, a very good mathematical model does not miss any of the data points used to generate it by much. However, it is also true that a good model does not create a pattern in its residuals—there should be a good deal of randomness in the way they are distributed. One very good way to check for patterns in residuals is to plot them sequentially, either above or below a horizontal axis, according to whether they are positive or negative.

Although there are many things about travel that I do not like, the time I spend on planes and in airports does give me a chance to catch up on some of the things for which I have difficulty finding time. So it was, that one day last fall I carried a new textbook I'd been wanting to examine and my TI–81 calculator aboard a plane to Washington, DC, determined that by the time we landed I'd have worked out a few enhancements for the data analysis portions of the classes I teach.

The textbook I carried aboard the plane was a new precalculus text written by the members of the mathematics department at the North Carolina School of Science and Mathematics. It places heavy emphasis on data analysis. I took my TI–81 calculator because I wanted a residual plot program and knew it would not be difficult to write. As the plane took off, I grabbed my notepad and calculator and began working on the program (**Figure 1**).

```
Clrdraw
All-Off
0→Xmin
Dim{x}+1→Xmax
1→Xscl
0→Yscl
100000→M
–100000→N
1→K
Lbl 1
{x}(K)→X
If {y}(K)–Y₁>N
{y}(K)–Y₁→N
If {y}(K)–Y₁<M
{y}(K)–Y₁→M
IS>(K,Dim{x})
Goto 1
N+.05(N–M)→Ymax
M–.05(N–M)→Ymin
1→K
Lbl 2
{x}(K)→X
{y}(K)–Y₁→Y
Pt-Chg(K,Y)
IS>(K,Dim{x})
Goto 2
```

FIGURE 1. TI–81 RESIDUAL PLOT PROGRAM.

To use the program, first store the data in the calculator's statistical memory, then store the model as Y_1. When the program is run, a plot of the residuals appears on the screen.

Pressing one of the cursor keys places on the screen a moving cursor and readout that may be used to estimate the size of the residuals. If a residual is close to zero, and thereby on the axis or one of the tic marks, the program plots it in white rather than in black, so that it appears as a gap in the axis or tic mark.

Academic Year	Total Cost
1975	$4205
1976	4460
1977	4680
1978	4960
1979	5510
1980	6060
1981	6845
1982	7600
1983	8435
1984	9000
1985	9659

FIGURE 2. PRIVATE COLLEGE COSTS.

Once the program was written, I browsed through the North Carolina text looking for a data set to test it against. I found a table of college costs for private colleges that was taken from *The College Board News* (**Figure 2**). I entered the data into the TI–81 (leaving off the first two digits of the year), ran the calculator's linear regression routine, entered the model as Y_1, set a viewing rectangle of [70, 90] x [4000, 10000], and ordered a scatter plot (**Figure 3**). The data, I noticed, seemed to oscillate about the line. I then ran the residual plot program, thus magnifying the effect (**Figure 4**).

The program's plot matched that of the textbook, thus it was working correctly. The almost sinusoidal pattern to the residuals indicated that the linear regression model, $y = 575.55x - 39,551$, although it carried a very high correlation coefficient, was flawed. I tried the calculator's exponential, logarithmic, and power function models with similar results.

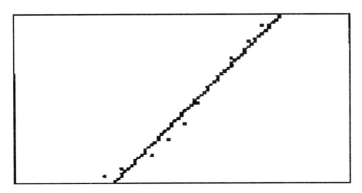

FIGURE 3. THE DATA AND THE TI–81'S LINEAR MODEL.

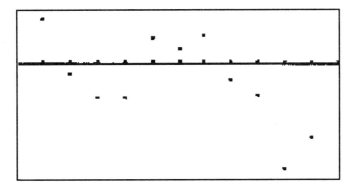

FIGURE 4. [0, 12] × [–483, 642].

The results intrigued me, and I soon felt like one of my students, playing the computer game *Algebra Arcade*, trying to find a function that would hit as many "algebroids" as possible. Moving the cursor around the residual plot had given me approximate maximum and minimum values, cycle length, and phase displacement for the nearly sinusoidal pattern. I added the function –500 sin $((2\pi/10)(x - 77))$ to the linear model already stored in the calculator and ordered another residual plot (**Figure 5**).

Although the cursor readout showed that the size of the residuals had diminished, the oscillating pattern of the residuals was still somewhat apparent. I wondered what would happen if I further enhanced the model by forcing the trigonometric portion to better approximate the high and low values of the residuals. I used the cursor to find approximate values of three residuals: 600 at 75, 450 at 79.5, and 285 at 85. Three points always determine a quadratic, $ax^2 + bx + c$. What, I wondered, would happen if I used the quadratic that fit these three points to modify my model?

I solved the system $75^2a + 75b + c = 600$; $79.5^2a + 79.5b + c = 450$; $85^2a + 85b + c = 285$ by entering the coefficients as matrix A on the TI–81, the constants as matrix B, and calculating $[A]^{-1} * [B]$. The quadratic that resulted was $0.333x^2 - 84.83x + 5,087.5$. I then replaced the 500 in the trigonometric portion of the model with the quadratic. My model now consisted of the original linear regression model plus a trig function that had been multiplied by a quadratic.

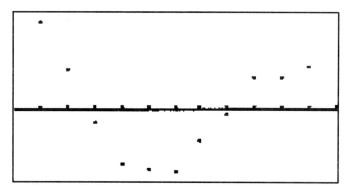

Figure 5. [0, 12] × [−289, 134].

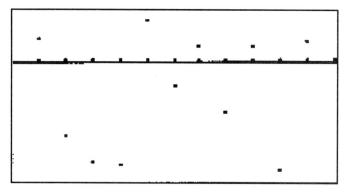

Figure 6. [0, 12] × [−97, 41].

Anxiously, I pressed the PRGM key and ordered a residual plot (**Figure 6**). The residuals appeared much more randomly distributed than in any of the previous attempts. No doubt, I thought, there could be no end to this refining process, but I was satisfied that I had developed a program that would be a useful tool for my students and also stumbled upon a problem that would provide interesting challenges as they learned to use mathematics to understand the world around them. ❑

REFERENCES

Foerster, Paul A. 1987. *Precalculus with Trigonometry.* Menlo Park, CA: Addison-Wesley.

Froelich, Gary W., Kevin G. Bartkovich and Paul A. Foerster. 1991. *Connecting Mathematics.* Reston, VA: NCTM.

Landwehr, James M. and Ann E. Watkins. 1986. *Exploring Data.* Palo Alto, CA: Dale Seymour.

Moore, David S. and George P. McCabe. 1989. *Introduction to the Practice of Statistics.* New York: W. H. Freeman.

North Carolina School of Science and Mathematics. 1991. *Contemporary Precalculus through Applications.* Providence, RI: Janson Publications.

SUMMER 1992

ANDREW RYSAVY
GARY FROELICH

Hot Dogs in a Box

Boxplots on the TI–81

Since its appearance two years ago, the TI–81 has had widespread acceptance in American high schools. Its programming features have helped create that acceptance. When my student Andrew expressed an interest in writing a boxplot program, I encouraged him. I knew from the tanks and other arcade-like characters I'd seen animated on his TI–81 screen that he was a capable programmer.

Andrew started with a basic program that drew a single boxplot. Boxplots, however, are normally used for comparisons of several sets of data, so I asked him to develop a loop that would draw several on the same screen. With this accomplished, he worked on shortening the program as much as possible to make its use more practical.

A statistical boxplot is merely a rectangle whose ends represent the lower and upper quartiles of a data set. The segment near the center of the box represents the median. The box represents the middle 50% of the data, while the segments extending from each end of the box represent the lower 25% and the upper 25% of the data. These segments are sometimes referred to as *whiskers*, which accounts for the longer title of *box-and-whiskers-plots* that is sometimes used. (See Landwehr and Watkins [1986].)

Some people prefer to distinguish any member of the set that is over 1.5 boxlengths beyond either end of the box as an *outlier*. Andrew's program shows outliers as single pixels and does not extend the whiskers to reach them.

Not everyone uses the same method for finding the quartiles in a data set containing an even number of items. Some include the median in the halves of the data it creates, others don't. Andrew's program does not. The use of one method or another, however, has little if any effect on the appearance of the boxes.

Andrew's program is shown in **Figure 1**. **Figure 2** displays information on the calorie content of hot dogs of three types taken from the June, 1986 issue of *Consumer Reports* (see Moore and McCabe [1989]). The remaining **Figures** (**3** through **7**) show a sequence of steps that produces the boxplots on the TI–81 screen. The resulting boxes clearly demonstrate that the poultry hot dogs as a group have fewer calories than the other two types.

```
All-Off                End                    ({x}(G)+{x}(G+1))/2→C
ClrHome                Disp "DATA"            1.5(C–A)→F
ClrDraw                Lbl C                  A–F→D
Disp "MIN"             Input X                0→G
Input Xmin             If X<Xmin              Lbl E
Disp "MAX"             Goto A                 G+1→G
Input Xmax             T+1→T                  PT–On({x}(G),2S–.5)
Disp "MARKS"           X→{x}(T)               If {x}(G)<D
Input Xscl             Goto C                 Goto E
Disp "SETS"            Lbl A                  {x}(G)→D
Input R                Xsort                  T+1→G
0→S                    T/4→A                  C+F→E
0→Yscl                 T/2→B                  Lbl G
2R+1→Ymax              3A+.25→H               G–1→G
–.11Ymax→Ymin          IPart A→C              PT–On({x}(G),2S–.5)
Ymax-Ymin→C            IPart B→D              If {x}(G)>E
Ymin→X                 FPart A→E              Goto G
Lbl 1                  FPart B→F              {x}(G)→E
PT-Off(0,X)            IPart H→G              2S–1→F
X+C/70→X               FPart H→H              Line (A,F,C,F)
If X<Ymax              {x}(D+1)→B             Line (A,F+1,C,F+1)
Goto 1                 If F=0                 Line (A,F,A,F+1)
Line (0,0,0,C/50)      ({x}(D+1)+{x}(D))/2→B  Line (B,F,B,F+1)
Lbl B                  {x}(C+1)→A             Line (C,F,C,F+1)
ClrHome                If E<.4                Line (D,F+.5,A,F+.5)
ClrStat                ({x}(C)+{x}(C+1))/2→A  Line (E,F+.5,C,F+.5)
0→T                    {x}(G+1)→C             Goto B
S+1→S                  If H<.4
If S>R
```

FIGURE 1. ANDREW'S PROGRAM.

BEEF	MEAT	POULTRY
186	173	129
181	191	132
176	182	102
149	190	106
184	172	94
190	147	102
158	146	87
139	139	99
175	175	170
148	136	113
152	179	135
111	153	142
141	107	86
153	195	143
190	135	152
157	140	146
131	138	144
149		
135		
132		

FIGURE 2. CALORIE CONTENT OF HOT DOGS BY TYPE.

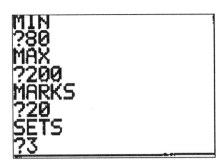

FIGURE 3. VALUES SLIGHTLY
BEYOND THE SMALLEST AND
LARGEST DATA ARE GIVEN
FOR MIN AND MAX. TIC-MARK
SPACING IS GIVEN AS 20
UNITS AND 3 SETS OF DATA
ARE SPECIFIED.

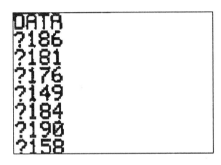

FIGURE 4. ENTRY OF THE
FIRST SET OF DATA BEGINS.

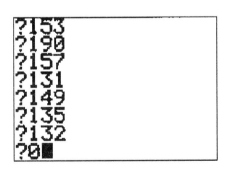

FIGURE 5. COMPLETION OF
THE FIRST SET OF DATA IS
SIGNALLED BY A VALUE
SMALLER THAN MIN. IN THIS
CASE, 0 IS USED, BUT
ANYTHING SMALLER THAN
80 WOULD WORK.

[*Andrew Rysavy authored the following portion of the article.*]

Recently, in my probability and statistics class, we were given an assignment involving boxplots. The tedium of number crunching prompted me to design a program for my TI–81 graphing calculator to find the medians and quartiles. From there, I decided to use the TI–81's graphing capabilities to have it display the boxplot. In order to make it useful, however, it needed to be able to display several of them at once.

With some help from my teacher, Mr. Froelich, who pointed out parts of the program that weren't needed, and with some careful rewriting of long sections, I was able to take nearly 300 bytes off of my original program.

To run the program, you must first find the high and low values of all the data in all the sets. Enter these as MAX and MIN when asked for them. These set the range, so if you want a special range, put appropriate values in for MAX and MIN instead. When asked for MARKS,

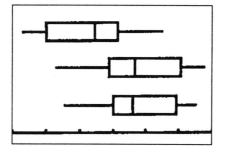

Figure 6. After completing the entry of the remaining two sets, the boxes are displayed by pressing [graph]. The lowest box represents the first set of data; the highest represents the last.

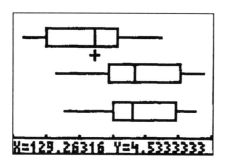

X=129.26316 Y=4.5333333

Figure 7. Pressing one of the calculator's cursor keys places on the screen a cursor that may be moved to read approximate values. In this case, the cursor indicates a median of about 129 for the third set of data. (The *y*-coordinate is meaningless.)

input the distance you want between the *x*-axis tic marks. When asked for sets, input the number of sets of data to be entered.

The data prompt indicates that you should begin entering the first set of data one item at a time. When you are done with a set, enter a number smaller than what you entered for min. You will then be asked to enter the next set of data in a similar way. When the program is done, hit the graph key to see the boxplots. If you need medians and quartiles, use the arrow keys to read the approximate values from the boxes.

REFERENCES

Landwehr, James M. and Ann E. Watkins. 1986. *Exploring Data*. Palo Alto, CA: Dale Seymour.

Moore, David S. and George P. McCabe. 1989. *Introduction to the Practice of Statistics*. New York: W.H. Freeman.

SPRING 1993

GARY FROELICH

Plots & Boxplots Revisited
Adapting TI–81 Programs for Casio Calculators

The Idea Exchange columns of *Consortium* 41 and 42 featured programs for the TI–81 graphing calculator that drew statistical residual plots and boxplots. Those columns brought comments from readers who requested similar programs for the Casio graphing calculators. In this article, we'll share several reader responses to those two columns.

Roger Pinkham of Stevens Institute of Technology in Hoboken, New Jersey, wrote about the residual plot column in *Consortium* 41. He commented on the program's treatment of the data as a time series and said that he sometimes needs to do residual plots when the domain elements are not equally spaced. Roger suggested changing the third

line from the bottom in the program from "Pt-Chg(K,Y)" to "Pt-Chg(X,Y)" and omitting the third, fourth and fifth lines, but noted that this requires that the range of values for X be set manually. A version of the program that does this automatically is shown in **Figure 1**.

One of my students, Doug Renton, translated the TI–81 residual plot program for his Casio. The program bases the residual plot on the function stored as f1. It is shown in **Figure 2**.

```
ClrDraw          {x}(K)→R
All-Off          If {x}(K)<Q
0→Xscl           {x}(K)→Q
0→Yscl           IS>(K,Dim{x})
100000→M         Goto 1
−100000→N        N+.05(N−M)→Ymax
100000→Q         M−.05(N−M)→Ymin
−100000→R        R+.05(R−Q)→Xmax
1→K              Q−.05(R−Q)→Xmin
Lbl 1            1→K
{x}(K)→X         Lbl 2
If {y}(K)−Y₁>N   {x}(K)→X
{y}(K)−Y₁→N      {y}(K)−Y₁→Y
If {y}(K)−Y₁<M   Pt−Chg(X,Y)
{y}(K)−Y₁→M      IS>(K,Dim{x})
If {x}(K)>R      Goto 2
```

FIGURE 1. REVISED RESIDUAL PLOT PROGRAM FOR THE TI–81.

```
"RESIDUAL"        Lbl 9
Cls               Z[N]→X
Defm 40           Z[O]−f₁>F⇒Z[O]−f₁→F
1→N               Z[O]−f₁<E⇒Z[O]−f₁→E
0→T               Z[N]>H⇒Z[N]→H
0→O               Z[N]<G⇒Z[N]→G
0→S               Isz N
"NUMBER OF        Isz O
ITEMS"?→I         N<I+1⇒Goto 9
Lbl 1             F+.07(F−E)→J
"X DATA"?Z→[N]    E−.07(F−E)→K
Isz N             H+.07(H−G)→L
N≤I⇒Goto 1        G−.07(H−G)→M
Lbl 2             Range M,L,C,K,J,D
"Y DATA"?→Z[N]    1→N
Isz N             I+1→O
N≤2I⇒Goto 2       1→K
Cls               Lbl 8
1→N               Z[N]→X
I+1→O             Z[N]→V
0→C               Z[O]−f₁→R
0→D               Plot V,R
100000→E          Isz N
−100000→F         Isz O
100000→G          N<I+1⇒Goto 8
−100000→H         Plot 0,0
1→K
```

FIGURE 2. DOUG RENTON'S RESIDUAL PLOT PROGRAM FOR CASIO.

```
"BOX"                          G+1→G
Cls                            Plot Z[G],2S-.5
Defm 20                        Z[G]<D⇒Goto 5
"MIN"                          Z[G]→D
?→L                            T+1→G
"MAX"                          C+F→E
?→H                            Lbl 6
"MARKS"                        G-1→G
?→K                            Plot Z[G],2S-.5
"SETS"                         Z[G]>E⇒Goto 6
?→R                            Z[G]→E
0→S                            2S-1→F
2R+1→W                         Plot A,F
-.11W→V                        Plot C,F
W-V→C                          Line
V→Q                            Plot A,F+1
Range L,H,K,V,W,0              Plot C,F+1
Plot 0,0                       Line
Plot 0,C÷50                    Plot A,F
Line                           Plot A,F+1
Lbl 2                          Line
0→T                            Plot B,F
S+1→S                          Plot B,F+1
S>R⇒Goto 7                     Line
"DATA"                         Plot C,F
Lbl 3                          Plot C,F+1
?→Q                            Line
Q<L⇒Goto 4                     Plot D,F+.5
T+1→T                          Plot A,F+.5
Q→Z[T]                         Line
Goto 3                         Plot E,F+.5
Lbl 4                          Plot C,F+.5
Prog 4                         Line
T÷4→A                          Goto 2
T÷2→B                          Lbl 7
3A+.25→H
Int(A)→C
Int(B)→D                       SUBROUTINE STORED
Frac(A)→E                      AS PROGRAM 4
Frac(B)→F
Int(H)→G
Frac(H)→H                      T-1→M
Z[D+1]→B                       Lbl 8
F=0⇒(Z[D+1]+Z[D])÷2            1→I
  →B                           M→J
Z[C+1]→A                       Lbl 9
E<.4⇒(Z[C]+Z[C+1])÷2           Z[I]<Z[I+1]⇒Goto 1
  →A                           Z[I+1]→N
Z[G+1]→C                       Z[I]→Z[I+1]
H<.4⇒(Z[G+1]+Z[G])÷            N→Z[I]
2→C                            Lbl 1
1.5(C-A)→F                     I+1→I
A-F→D                          Dsz J
0→G                            Goto 9
Lbl 5                          Dsz M
                               Goto 8
```

FIGURE 3. JOSEPH CIEPLY'S CASIO VERSION OF ANDREW RYSAVY'S BOXPLOT PROGRAM.

Doug's version differs substantially from the TI–81 version. Because of the proliferation of modes on the Casio and the walls that exist between them, the program requires the user to enter the data each time a residual plot is wanted. All the first members of the pairs are entered first, followed by the second members. Once the program terminates, the user can obtain a moving cursor for coordinate readouts by issuing a PLOT command.

Jim Sandefur of the National Science Foundation and Georgetown University commented in a conversation that enhancing the trigonometric model with a polynomial, as was done in the same column, is a fairly realistic procedure, but that statisticians often use an exponential function rather than a polynomial for this purpose.

Finally, several readers wrote wondering about a Casio version of Andrew Rysavy's boxplot program in *Consortium* 42's Idea Exchange. One reader, Joseph Cieply of Melrose Park, Illinois, kindly sent his Casio translation of the program, which is shown in **Figure 3**. It uses a separate subroutine for sorting that is shown immediately after the main program. Both columns included several references that are excellent resources on statistical graphs. An additional resource not given in either column is

Cleveland, William S. 1985. *The Elements of Graphing Data*. Monterey, CA: Wadsworth.

Thanks to Roger, Doug, Jim, and Joseph for sharing their ideas with the Idea Exchange. ❏

Section 4

The IBM *Mathematics Exploration Toolkit* (MET) is both a graphing utility and a symbolic manipulator. This combination makes it a much more powerful mathematical utility than those that offer only the first feature, as the articles in this section show. While the demonstrations are all done on MET, the ideas are adaptable to many other software packages and graphing calculators.

SPRING 1988

DR. JEFFREY GORDON

MET: The Symbolic Manipulator/Function Grapher

The Ultimate Tool for Teaching Mathematics

Editor's Note: *The position papers of the NCTM, AAAS, and MSEB (presently in draft form and soon to be published) indicates that software of the type discussed in this article will be a major factor in the improvement of our nation's mathematics curriculum. It is my understanding that the manufacturer of this software was to have it commercially available in January 1988. —Irwin Hoffman*

Sometimes teaching mathematics is not fun. Several years ago, I observed a student teacher attempting to teach the Fundamental Theorem of Algebra:

> *A polynomial expression of degree* n *has at most* n *real roots.*

His approach consisted of telling the students the theorem and then demonstrating it with a few first- and second-degree polynomials. I had the uneasy feeling that, as the students nodded along in agreement, the teacher could probably have convinced them that every polynomial had more than n real roots. The numbing fact is that students tend to believe whatever we tell them in mathematics, no matter how absurd.

Until recently, we have not had the tools at our disposal in secondary mathematics to really demonstrate key mathematical ideas in ways that the students can conceptually understand them. Our students typically memorize sets of procedures and calculation algorithms to be regurgitated back in virtually the identical form in which they were originally given the information.

As I began preparing for a high school mathematics course I am teaching, I found a piece of software from IBM that gives me the ability to actually instruct my students at the conceptual level. This software, called the *Mathematics Exploration Toolkit* (MET), runs on an IBM PC or PS/2. It can be used in conjunction with an LCD plate on an overhead projector to display the screen image to the entire class, or it can be used by individual students to explore mathematical ideas. This software allows me to use the computer in the manner expressed by the National Council of Teachers of Mathematics in its recommendations on the uses of computers in the mathematics classroom.

The *Mathematics Exploration Toolkit* solves equations; factors polynomials; graphs functions; creates domain/range tables within a specific domain; computes with matrices; extracts derivatives, integrals, and definite integrals; and has a built-in, easy-to-use macro language (essentially the existing commands in the software itself) so that the user can create commands for his or her own demonstrations.

Let's look at several examples from Algebra I and II using this software. I start by typing in the following equation: $y = x^2$. Now I can graph it in the function window by typing the command GRAPH. The graph appears almost instantly. With a few keystrokes, I now substitute $x - 3$ for x:

SUBST X – 3 X.

That's all it takes. The computer responds:

$y = (x - 3)^2$.

I can graph this new function by typing GRAPH. My students can now see that the new graph is the same as the old graph translated three units to the right. (See **Figure 1**.) I can call up the original graph, which i had stored, and this time I can substitute $x - 5$ for x. By typing GRAPH again, my students can see that the graph is offset five units to the right.

What if I wanted to translate the graph to the left? How could I do it? Now students can try out their own ideas and we can check them out immediately. I can ask my students to formulate a general translation rule in their own words and devise a plan for checking the rule out. After exploring with a number of substitutions, students can begin verbalizing the rules. Another example of an exercise would be to add and subtract a constant term and see what happens to the graph.

Once the students have explored with the coefficients and constants in a polynomial,

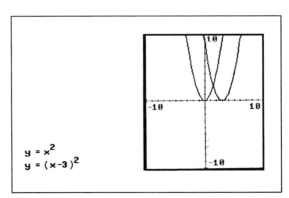

Figure 1. The graph of $y = (x - 3)^2$.

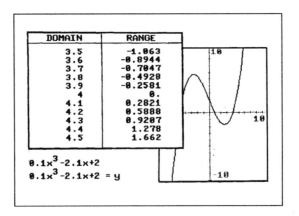

Figure 2. The graph of $0.1x^3 - 2.1x + 2$.

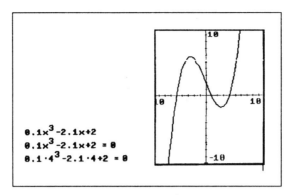

Figure 3. The graph of subst 4 x.

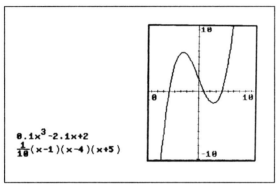

Figure 4. The graph of factor.

they begin to see the effects on the roots to the polynomial. For example, consider the following equation:

$$0.1x^3 - 2.1x + 2 = 0.$$

How many real solutions does this equation have? This type of equation is normally beyond the high school student's capacity to solve, because the arithmetic can become lengthy and tedious. With the *Mathematics Exploration Toolkit*, finding the solution set becomes incredibly easy.

My first step is to alter the equation:

$$0.1x^3 - 2.1x + 2 = y,$$

and then I type GRAPH to graph the equation. By observation, it appears that there are solutions when y is 0 at 1, 4, and –5, but to be more certain, I can zoom in on several of these points. The program also allows me to call up a domain/range of values. I request values between 4.5 and 3.5 and examine the y-value for 4 in that table. (See **Figure 2**.) This provides very convincing evidence that 4 is

indeed a solution, but I need to check it out further.

One approach would be to substitute 4 for x and see what happens to the graph. As before, I type

SUBST 4   X.

The screen then reads:

$$0.1 * 43 - 2.1 * 4 + 2 = y.$$

(See **Figure 3**.)

By typing SIMP (simplify), the screen reads:

$$0 = y.$$

I can quickly determine that the roots are 1, 4, and –5.

Now I can try another approach to the problem. I take my original polynomial $(0.1x^3 - 2.1 + 2)$ and factor it by typing FACTOR. The screen displays:

$$0.1(x - 1)(x - 4)(x + 5).$$

(See **Figure 4**.)

If all of the roots are integers (most that we deal with in algebra are), the program will factor the polynomial regardless of degree. Upon making the factored expression equal to zero, the program can automatically solve for x and arrive at the same solutions we determined earlier.

An alternative approach is for students to discover that if 4, for example, is a root of the original polynomial, then $(x - 4)$ must be able to divide into the polynomial.

Therefore, I can retrieve my original polynomial and type DIV x − 4 (which means to divide the existing polynomial by $x - 4$).

The computer screen responds:

$$\frac{0.1^*x^3 - 2.1x + 2}{x - 4}.$$

Typing SIMP yields: $0.1x^2 + 0.4x - 5$.

Since we now have a second-degree polynomial with no remainder, $x - 4$ must be a factor. Therefore, 4 must be a root of the original polynomial.

By solving polynomial expressions using a variety of approaches, students can begin to see that the solution approximations obtained through graphing match those obtained through a domain/range table and achieve the values when the polynomial is factored, provided it is factorable and divisible into integer solutions. Since these approaches all yield the same solutions, the algebraic relationships among these varied approaches become more apparent. My students can now really understand what the roots of a polynomial represent.

This software tool allows students to explore some interesting mathematical ideas, such as the implications of the Fundamental Theorem of Algebra. For example:

- How many real roots can a second-degree polynomial have?
- How many real roots will a second-degree polynomial have?
- How many real roots can a third-degree polynomial have?
- How many real roots will a third-degree polynomial have?
- How many real roots can an n-degree polynomial have?
- How many real roots will an n-degree polynomial have?
- Under what conditions will a polynomial of degree 2 have fewer than two real roots?

In addition to all of the features previously described, built into the *Mathematics Exploration Toolkit* is a macro language that allows the teacher or student to create his or her own individualized commands and features. A set of about 30 of these macros comes with the package. One macro demonstrates how to compute the Riemann Sum when calculating an integral. Not only is the result calculated, the function with the appropriate rectangles is automatically graphed on the screen. I am creating some applications of my own to demonstrate inequality relationship.

The *Mathematics Exploration Toolkit* gives me the tools needed to have my students examine fundamental mathematical relationships. This software provides me with the electronic chalkboard I have always wanted. No longer do I have to graph equations sloppily by hand. No longer do I have to avoid polynomials and functions with difficult-to-compute coefficients and constants. No longer do I have to worry about solutions that must come out "nice" in order to do the problem. I can spend my instructional time teaching mathematical ideas instead of dwelling on symbol manipulation techniques.

This year, teaching math is fun. ❑

FALL 1988

GARY FROELICH

The Toolkit

IBM's *Mathematics Exploration Toolkit*

In *Consortium* 25, both the Idea Exchange and Computers columns discussed computer software of the function grapher genre. In this article, we'll again visit the topics of those two columns

The Ohio State function plotter discussed in Idea Exchange is now available commercially from Addison-Wesley. The price for the Apple, IBM, or Macintosh version is $19.95. A separate three-dimensional plotter is available for IBM and Macintosh.

One reader, Dick Hanson of Burnsville, Minnesota, called to recommend a function plotter called *Epic*. The IBM program is available from Prentice-Hall for about $50. He prefers it to any other he has used, but emphasized it does not include the symbolic manipulator provided with IBM's *Mathematics Exploration Toolkit.*

The IBM *Toolkit* was the subject of the Computers column in *Consortium* 25. Although it is not being distributed at this writing, the *Toolkit* should be available by the time this column appears. [The program is now widely available.] IBM has trained a team of educators to provide *Toolkit* inservice at no cost to schools. Information can be obtained through local IBM representatives.

Dr. Irwin Hoffman, editor of the Computers column, is also a member of the IBM inservice team. I found him at the IBM display at the NCTM meeting in Chicago and was immediately attracted to a problem he and several others were tackling. It was to find all solutions of $2x = x^{10}$.

The reader will note that the usual logarithmic method does not free one of the variables. This, therefore, is a nice problem to tackle with a function plotter. If your students are using a function plotter, most would graph the functions $2x$ and x^{10} and look for intersections. **Figure 1** shows one such attempt done with the IBM *Toolkit*. There appear to be two solutions. Each solution can be estimated quite accurately by using the ZOOM and COORDINATE READOUT features of most function plotters.

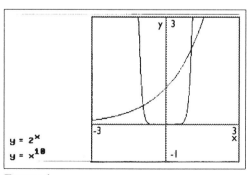

FIGURE 1.

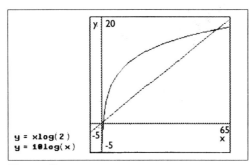

FIGURE 2.

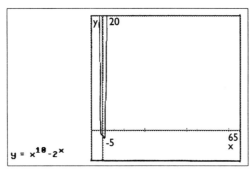

FIGURE 3.

Other students may first attempt the algebraic solution and then, stymied, switch to the plotter. **Figure 2** shows the graphs that result. Here again we see two solutions, but one of them is new! We cannot see the negative solution because $\log(x)$ is not defined for negatives.

Note that in Figure 2 the new solution is somewhat below 65. One might ask if this solution would appear if a large enough range of values had been graphed in Figure 1. The answer is no! The number 265 is beyond the machine's capabilities. The next challenge, then, is to find a way to show all three solutions simultaneously.

One promising idea is to form a difference equation, $x^{10} - 2x$, and look for its zeros. **Figure 3** shows this attempt. Note that the third solution does not appear. This seeming impossibility is clarified by considering values of the function and the plotting style of the computer. **Figure 4** shows a table of values for the difference equation. Note that even for values quite close to the zero, the differences are large. The connect-the-dots style graphing done by the software is left without two pixels to connect!

How are we to see all three solutions simultaneously? One method that works is to create a new function by forming the ratio of the two and watching for intersections with $y = 1$. Another is to form the function $x^{10}/2x - 1$ and look for zeros. **Figure 5** shows the result of the latter. At last we have met with success!

Computer and calculator function plotters are a powerful new problem-solving tool. With them, students can tackle non-standard problems, problems that they might not be able to solve mathematically without several additional years of study. Yet, as we have seen, computers and calculators have their limitations. As electronic aids become more commonplace our students will no doubt need to learn new problem-solving skills and strategies to help them adjust to these limitations.

No doubt many of you have used function plotters with students and found other unusual problems. Have you a problem that is particularly suitable for solving with a function plotter or that points out some limitation of the machine? Why not send them to the column editor? We'll discuss them in a future issue of *Consortium.* ❏

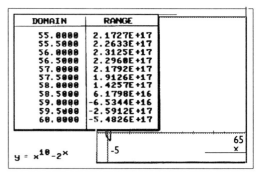

FIGURE 4.

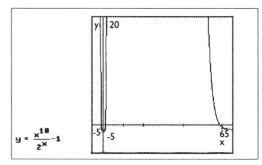

FIGURE 5.

Summer 1989

IRWIN HOFFMAN

Families of Circles

The software used for this article is the Mathematics Exploration Toolkit (MET) by IBM.

The addition and subtraction method is a process students use in first-year algebra to find the intersection of two lines. The students eliminate a variable by choosing appropriate multiples of the coefficients and then add or subtract the functions (a linear combination of the functions). This "algorithm" is then often extended to higher-order function. For instance, students might be encouraged to find the intersection of two circles using this method.

Suppose we look at the geometry of the linear combination of two circles and observe what happens in the general cases when the original circles intersect, are tangent, and when they have no points in common. It is interesting to examine the result of the special case where the linear combination eliminates the second degree terms.

I. Circles with a common secant or chord

1. MET allows us to designate a circle by inputting the center and the radius. **Figure 1** shows a circle with center at (–2, –5) and a radius of 4. The simplified expression is then stored in address *a*. The letter *a* can subsequently be used to represent the equation of the circle. In **Figure 2**, Circle (I – 2), a second circle with center (1, 2) and a radius of 6 is stored in address *b* and *b* will be the designation of this second circle.

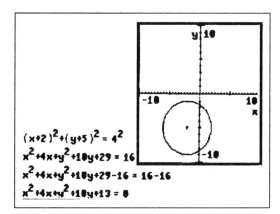

FIGURE 1. CIRCLE (I – 1).

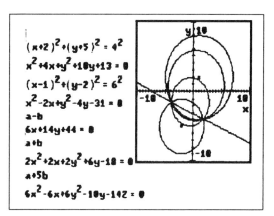

FIGURE 2. CIRCLE (I – 2).

2. Various linear combinations of circle *a* and circle *b* are found and graphed. The software allows us to indicate linear combinations of *a* and *b* and then replace the variables with the contents stored in these addresses. It is interesting that the simple combination *a – b* eliminates the second-degree terms of the circles stored in addresses *a* and *b*. The result of this subtraction is a linear equation. This is the equation of the secant line, which is common to the family of circles produced by the combination of circles *a* and *b*. (See Figure 2.)

3. In order to find the points of intersection of the secant line with the circles, one solves the equation of the secant line for *y* and substitutes that value into one of the circles. The resulting solution is shown in **Figure 3**.

4. One can take the values of *x* and substitute them into the equation of the secant line to obtain the corresponding values of *y*. (See **Figure 4**.)

5. The ordered pairs found in Figure 3 and Figure 4 determine the chord that is common to the family of circles. (See **Figure 5**.)

$$x^2+4x+y^2+10y+13 = 0$$
$$6x+14y+44 = 0$$
$$y = -\frac{3}{7}x-\frac{22}{7}$$
$$x^2+4x+\left(-\frac{3}{7}x-\frac{22}{7}\right)^2+10\left(-\frac{3}{7}x-\frac{22}{7}\right)+13 = 0$$
$$\frac{58}{49}x^2+\frac{118}{49}x-\frac{419}{49} = 0$$
$$x = \frac{-5782\sqrt{7}-43210}{5684\sqrt{7}}$$
$$x = \frac{-5782\sqrt{7}+43210}{5684\sqrt{7}}$$

FIGURE 3. CIRCLE (I – 3).

$$y = \frac{-3}{7}x-\frac{22}{7}$$
$$y = \frac{-3}{7}\left(\frac{-5782\sqrt{7}-43218}{5684\sqrt{7}}\right)-\frac{22}{7}$$
$$y = \frac{-3}{7}\cdot 1.8566-\frac{22}{7} = -3.9385$$
$$y = \frac{-3}{7}\left(\frac{-5782\sqrt{7}+43218}{5684\sqrt{7}}\right)-\frac{22}{7}$$
$$y = \frac{-3}{7}(-3.8911)-\frac{22}{7} = -1.475$$

FIGURE 4. CIRCLE (I – 4).

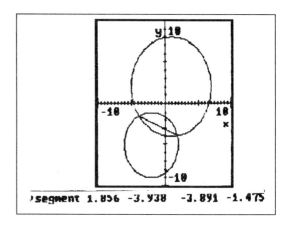

segment 1.856 -3.938   -3.891 -1.475

FIGURE 5. CIRCLE (I – 5).

II. FAMILY OF CIRCLES WITH A COMMON TANGENT

One can construct any two initial circles that are tangent to each other. In **Figure 6**, circle a has center at $(-1, 4)$ with a radius of 6 and circle b has center $(-1, 3)$ with a radius of 5. The linear combinations of these circles and their subsequent graphs show a family of circles tangent at the same point. Again, the simple combination of $a - b$ subtracts the second-degree terms and gives the linear equation, which is the tangent line.

III. CIRCLES THAT DON'T INTERSECT

1. If the two original circles don't intersect, then the combinations of these circles don't intersect. (See **Figure 7**.) In this example, Circle b has a center $(-2, 4)$ with a radius of 2. Circle a has a center $(-1, 3)$ and a radius of 5. The line produced by the combination $a - b$ does not intersect the circles.

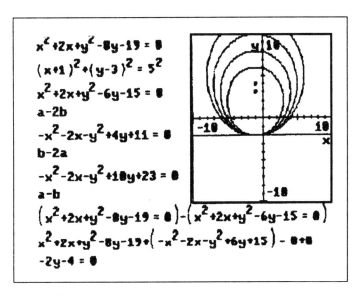

FIGURE 6. CIRCLE (II – 1).

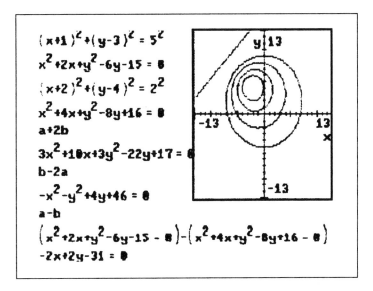

FIGURE 7. CIRCLE (III – 1).

2. Some linear combinations do not work. For instance, when one tries to graph the linear combination $a - 2b$, a message appears that nothing was graphed. This can be understood by looking at the discriminant of the solution for y that comes from the expression $a - 2b$. (See **Figure 8**.)

3. If one graphs the discriminant, it is obvious that it will never be positive. A table confirms the fact that there is no real value that allows for the circle $a - 2b$. (See **Figure 9**.) ❑

$$(x+1)^2+(y-3)^2 = 5^2$$

$$(x+2)^2+(y-4)^2 = 2^2$$

a-2b

$$x^2+2x+y^2-6y-15-2(x^2+4x+y^2-8y+16) = 0$$

$$-x^2-6x-y^2+10y-47 = 0$$

$$y = \frac{-10-\sqrt{100-(4x^2+24x+188)}}{-2}$$

$$y = \frac{-10+\sqrt{100-(4x^2+24x+188)}}{-2}$$

$$\sqrt{-4x^2-24x-88}$$

FIGURE 8. CIRCLE (III – 2).

DOMAIN	RANGE
10.0000	240.0000
8.0000	152.0000
-6.0000	-88.0000
-4.0000	-56.0000
-2.0000	-56.0000
0.0000	-88.0000
2.0000	-152.0000
4.0000	-248.0000
6.0000	-376.0000
8.0000	-536.0000
10.0000	720.0000

$$\sqrt{-4x^2-24x-88}$$

$4x^2$ 24x 88 - y

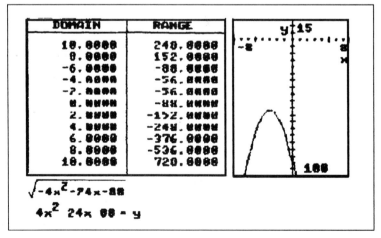

FIGURE 9. CIRCLE (III – 3).

FALL 1992

PATSY MCDONALD

Get with the Programming!

Surviving Computer Mathematics Using the *Mathematics Exploration Toolkit*

This Computers column gives an example of the kind of programming that is available to students today. The teaching of the basics of programming is still important, even though more and more schools are getting away from teaching traditional programming languages. The defers of the Mathematics Exploration Toolkit *(MET) provide students with a means to learn those basics.*
—Irwin Hoffman, Editor.

The Texas Essential Elements for the Computer Mathematics courses include programming in languages such as BASIC, COBOL, FORTRAN, and Pascal; and they provide opportunities for students to use the computer to solve problems related to specified topics in mathematics, science, economics, and business. Now, I no longer believe that the students should have to write the programs to solve ALL of these problems. Since the *Mathematics Exploration Toolkit* (MET) is very appropriate for many of these topics, I wanted to use it as much as possible. Unfortunately, I received it the week classes started, so we started the old way—solving problems by writing programs.

When we finally started working with MET around Thanksgiving (I still hadn't had much time to spend on it), one of their first questions was "When can we start writing our own defers?" Well, I bought some time, but now what could I do without working myself to death?

Anyone who is familiar with the power of MET can see how to tell students to use it to solve problems; however, writing defers that are significant and nontrivial is another question. In mild panic and self-defense, I studied the defers that came with MET, and discovered some excellent programming techniques. Deciding this would be a good way for the students to learn some solid techniques in writing interactive defers, I came up with their first assignment: randomly generate the endpoints of a segment (using the CIRCLE defer as a model) and respond appropriately to the user's computation of the midpoint.

I have now received several defers on topics chosen by the students and based on their diverse mathematical experience: randomly generate the vertices of a triangle for the user to compute its area; randomly generate the graph of a sine curve for the user to correctly identify the equation; and generate the graphs of sine and cosine curves in polar coordinates. One defer that rates further discussion is an application of a physics lab on graphical analysis of motion that demonstrates the differentiation, integration, and graphing capabilities of MET. It was written by a senior, Thomas Wells, and generates displacement, acceleration, and velocity graphs from input velocity data. (See samples codes in **Figures 1** and **2**. Be sure to first store the given velocities as u, v, w, x, y and z before running DEFER B.)

Sequence 'B' assumes the initial displacement at $t = 0$ to be 0, then computes the displacements by integrating velocities over their respective time intervals, and stores the accumulative displacements in a, b, c, d, f, and g. Sequence 'VEL' is then executed.

```
DEFER B              c+d
show off             replace
0                    simplify
store a              store d
B(t)+u               F(t–3)+x
replace              replace
defint 0 1 t         defint 3 4 t
simplify             simplify
simplify             simplify
store b              store f
C(t–1)+v             d+f
replace              replace
defint 1 2 t         simplify
simplify             store f
simplify             G(t–4)+y
store c              replace
b+c                  defint 4 5 t
replace              simplify
simplify             simplify
store c              store g
D(t–2)+w             f+g
replace              replace
defint 2 3 t         simp
simplify             store g
simplify             run VEL
store d              stop
```

FIGURE 1. THE FIRST SEGMENT OF THE PROGRAM.

Sequence 'VEL' graphs the velocity segments in magenta (color 2), with vertical lines in white (color 3) for easy reference. The user is given the option of regraphing the velocity with changed limits or continuing with the execution of 'DISPL'.

```
DEFER VEL
clr e
clr f
label y VELOCITY
label x TIME (sec)
text           VELOCITY
color 3
segment 1 0 1 v
segment 2 0 2 w
segment 3 0 3 x
segment 4 0 4 y
segment 5 0 5 z
color 2
segment 0 u 1 v
segment 1 v 2 w
segment 2 w 3 x
segment 3 x 4 y
segment 4 y 5 z
show on
write Velocities for
write 0,1,2,3,4,5 sec:
show off
write [u],[v],[w]∫,[x],[y],[z].
show on
replace
write
write You may change the
write limits by entering
write \Clims –1 6 –y1 y2
write then \CRUN VEL\W to
write regraph, or continue
write with \MRUN DISPL\W.
stop
```

FIGURE 2. THE SECOND SEGMENT OF THE PROGRAM.

The velocity graph (**Figure 3**) is approximated by straight-line segments defined by the ordered pairs $(0, u)$, $(1, v)$, $(2, w)$, $(3, x)$, $(4, y)$, and $(5, z)$. During any given second, the velocity graph passes through the points (t_0, V_0) and (t_f, V_f), and $t_f - t_0 = 1$, so the slope $m = V_f - V_0$ defines the acceleration during that second. Motion during the first second is defined by the velocity segment from $(0, u)$ to $(1, v)$ and its slope, $v - u$, is stored as ACCELERATION B. During the next second for the velocity segment from $(1, v)$ to $(2, w)$, $w - v$, its slope, is stored as ACCELERATION C, and so on. In this manner, the accelerations during the first five seconds are stored in B, C, D, F, and G, and the acceleration graph (**Figure 4**) is defined

by the segments from $(0, B)$ to $(1, B)$, from $(1, C)$ to $(2, C)$, from $(2, D)$ to $(3, D)$, from $(3, F)$ to $(4, F)$, and from $(4, G)$ to $(5, G)$. On the screen, the 0 acceleration is visible because of the color.

During each second, the velocity graph passes through the points (t_0, V_0) and (t_f, V_f) and its equation is $V = m(t - t_0) + V_0$, where $m = V_f - V_0$. The displacements are calculated during each second by integrating the velocity $V(t)$ from t_0 to t_f. An initial displacement of 0 is stored in a. Motion during the first second is defined by the the velocity segment from $(0, u)$ to $(1, v)$ with slope B, so the velocity function $B(t - 0) + u$ is integrated from 0 to 1 with respect to t to obtain b, the total

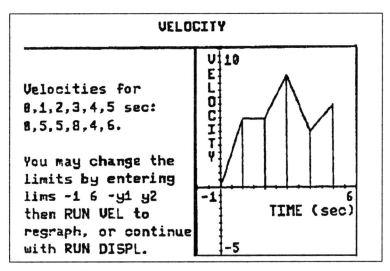

FIGURE 3. THE VELOCITY GRAPH.

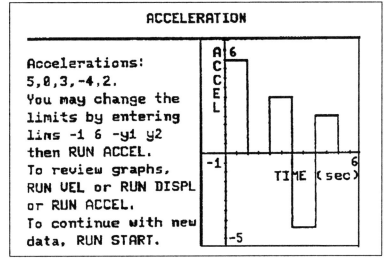

FIGURE 4. THE ACCELERATION GRAPH.

displacement after 1 second. During the next second for the velocity segment from $(1, v)$ to $(2, w)$ with slope C, the velocity function $C(t - 1) + v$ is integrated from 1 to 2 with respect to t to obtain the displacement during that second. The previous displacement b is added to that value to obtain c, the total displacement after two seconds. Continuing in this manner, the displacements are stored in a, b, c, d, f, and g, and the ordered pairs on the displacement graph (**Figure 5**) are represented by $(0, a)$, $(1, b)$, $(2, c)$, $(3, d)$, $(4, f)$, and $(5, g)$.

I am excited about using the language of the application software to fulfill some of the programming requirements for the course. Of course, MET won't do everything, so we fall back on writing Pascal programs to extend concepts (like solving systems of equations up to seven equations in seven unknowns by matrix methods using row reduction "commands"). The students have had fun programming with MET, and with relatively little work on my part, I have obtained some excellent defers (and Pascal programs) that can be used in other classes by other teachers.

If you wish a copy of the entire article, which includes the full set of programs that will generate Figures 4 and 5 (WordPerfect 5.1 file), send a stamped, self-addressed envelope and a formatted disk (I have 5.25" and 3.5" HD drives) to me at 2201 Highway 1431 West #22, Marble Falls, TX 78654. ❏

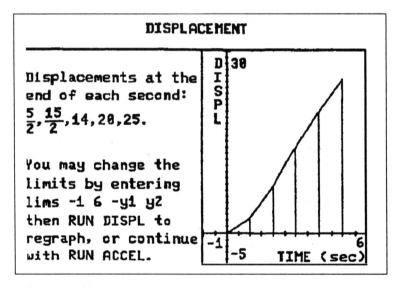

FIGURE 5. THE DISPLACEMENT GRAPH.

WINTER 1992

LISA WILLIAMS

The House of Math Magic

This article illustrates how technology can be used to enhance the mathematical experiences of young students. Most applications that appear in the Computers column are for more advanced students, so it is a pleasure to bring you these examples. —Eds.

October brought an exciting event to my math classes last year. In keeping with the Halloween spirit, I designed a math lesson that would incorporate a review of previously learned objectives, as well as introduce future topics, using a totally different format involving "Math Magic" and the *Mathematics Exploration Toolkit* (MET) software. The student teacher and I enjoyed the presentation as much as the students did, and we are excited to be able to share this idea with other math teachers.

We heard that old familiar bell telling us it was time to go to Algebra. We went into the hall and over to the door but it was locked. In an instant, the doorknob moved and the door slowly opened. We could scarcely see inside. We entered the black, eerie cavern we commonly knew as room 208, Algebra II. Who was that ugly witch under the large, black, pointed hat beckoning us to come in? The gross nose with the large wart did not give us a clue. Black dress, black cape, and black shoes were not the attire of the woman who usually welcomed us with news of properties, definitions, and axioms to explore each day.

The room was lit with only the glow of a jack-o-lantern in the distant corner and a projected message on the wall. We could hear the frightening sounds of a haunted house while fog filled the front of the room, where an escaped convict hid behind a large, black object. We ducked to miss the spider web as we entered the room and groped our way to our chairs. When all students had arrived, the witch proclaimed that

"Where we are going today, no one needs books! Put away all books!"

We were in shock. What are we going to do today in Algebra?

The message projected on the wall read: "What is MET?" We could not solve the mystery of the acronym. The witch began her spell by introducing us to MET, the *Mathematics Exploration Toolkit*. She explained that MET would be questioning us on mathematical concepts we had already learned; it would take us into the future and let us get a glimpse of concepts yet to be discovered.

The escaped convict (my teaching assistant, Chris Billings), wearing striped garments with ball and chain, seemed to control the messages on the wall. At times, the view of him was obscured by the large, black object (this was the computer hidden by a large black cloth so the students couldn't see the source of the magic).

MET began its task by flashing mathematical problems on the wall for us to solve. The problem to be solved might involve using the properties or laws of rational exponents or it might ask us to solve a system of linear equations. (See **Figures 1** and **2**.) Each correct answer was rewarded with a treat from the witch's or convict's goodie bag. We worked hard for those treats. The witch did not allow any student to escape MET's snare. Problem-solving skills were sharpened on problems such as finding the area of the Bermuda Triangle given its height is 9,000 caskets and its base is 11,000 caskets.

The questioning by MET was interrupted occasionally by the witch and convict performing some real magic tricks. Can you balance two forks on the edge of a jar with a quarter? How can the convict bounce a small, black ball so high that it would hit the metal rafter but we could not make it bounce at all?

Can you imagine that our wish would come true if we would hit these two rocks together with all might? We did not expect the sparks and loud pop to occur with our wish! Oh yes, we worked so hard to get the two twisted, metal puzzle pieces apart so that we might receive another treat from the bag.

THE DEFERS IN FIGURES 1 THROUGH 3 HAVE FREQUENT "PAUSE LINES" TO ALLOW THE TEACHER TO CONTROL MOVEMENT TO THE NEXT LINE. THE RETURN KEY MUST BE HIT IN ORDER FOR THE PROGRAM TO CONTINUE. DURING THESE PAUSES, QUESTIONING TECHNIQUES WERE USED TO MONITOR STUDENT PERFORMANCE AND ENCOURAGE THE USE OF HIGHER-LEVEL THINKING SKILLS (AS WELL AS INCORPORATE THE SPIRIT OF HALLOWEEN). YOU CAN BE AS CREATIVE AS YOU WISH! MANY "WRITE LINES" WERE USED SO THAT THE TEXT DISPLAYED ON THE SCREEN WOULD BE EASIER TO READ.

```
Defer Rational Ex1
CLR E CLR F
Write Simplify this expression using the
   properties of rational exponents.
Write
Pause
Write 3^(1/2)*3^(3/5)=
Pause
Write What is the rule or property for this
   problem?
Pause
Write Did you get 3^(11/10)?
Pause
```

```
Write Let's try another.
Write
Write What about this one?
Write (9^(3/5))^(2/3) =
Write What is the rule or property for this
   problem?
Pause
Write Did you get 9^(2/5)?
Pause
Stop
Save Rational Ex1
```

FIGURE 1. THE RATIONAL EXPONENT DEFER.

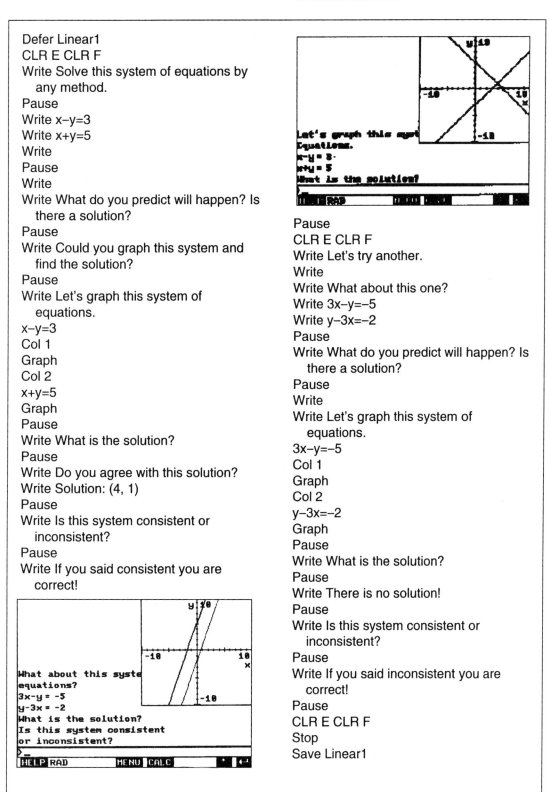

Defer Linear1
CLR E CLR F
Write Solve this system of equations by
    any method.
Pause
Write x−y=3
Write x+y=5
Write
Pause
Write
Write What do you predict will happen? Is
    there a solution?
Pause
Write Could you graph this system and
    find the solution?
Pause
Write Let's graph this system of
    equations.
x−y=3
Col 1
Graph
Col 2
x+y=5
Graph
Pause
Write What is the solution?
Pause
Write Do you agree with this solution?
Write Solution: (4, 1)
Pause
Write Is this system consistent or
    inconsistent?
Pause
Write If you said consistent you are
    correct!

Pause
CLR E CLR F
Write Let's try another.
Write
Write What about this one?
Write 3x−y=−5
Write y−3x=−2
Pause
Write What do you predict will happen? Is
    there a solution?
Pause
Write
Write Let's graph this system of
    equations.
3x−y=−5
Col 1
Graph
Col 2
y−3x=−2
Graph
Pause
Write What is the solution?
Pause
Write There is no solution!
Pause
Write Is this system consistent or
    inconsistent?
Pause
Write If you said inconsistent you are
    correct!
Pause
CLR E CLR F
Stop
Save Linear1

FIGURE 2. THE LINEAR DEFER.

Now it was time to answer more difficult questions posed by MET. We all had our share of problems to solve; then it was time to get a glance into the future. Those of us who were brave decided to gaze into the crystal ball. Sparks were flying everywhere and we passed the shocks onto the person next to us. MET's power was unleashed! What a dazzling display of power! We had never seen such colorful graphing. We were amazed to see the graphs of equations involving absolute values. As MET changed the equations, we

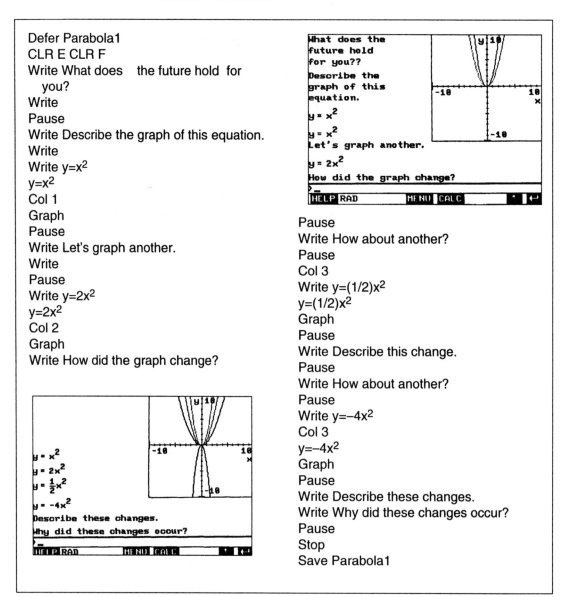

```
Defer Parabola1
CLR E CLR F
Write What does   the future hold  for
    you?
Write
Pause
Write Describe the graph of this equation.
Write
Write y=x²
y=x²
Col 1
Graph
Pause
Write Let's graph another.
Write
Pause
Write y=2x²
y=2x²
Col 2
Graph
Write How did the graph change?
```

```
Pause
Write How about another?
Pause
Col 3
Write y=(1/2)x²
y=(1/2)x²
Graph
Pause
Write Describe this change.
Pause
Write How about another?
Pause
Write y=−4x²
Col 3
y=−4x²
Graph
Pause
Write Describe these changes.
Write Why did these changes occur?
Pause
Stop
Save Parabola1
```

FIGURE 3. THE PARABOLA DEFER.

predicted the results. We really stepped into the future when we saw the graphs of conic sections! (See **Figure 3**.)

What, the sound of a bell. We were bounced back into reality. Our trip into the haunted house (or room 208) was over. What time is it? What are we to do? Where are we to go? Oh yes, it is time for second period and we must leave the dark cavern to enter the bright lights of the hall. What a trip! We will never forget the House of Math Magic! ❑

Spring 1993

DOUG BRUMBAUGH

Showing How Mathematicians Think

NCTM's *Standards, Everybody Counts*, and *Reshaping the Schools* all call for teachers of mathematics to show students how mathematicians think and to encourage problem solving. Especially when we use the computer as a teaching tool, so many exciting opportunities present themselves to aid in meeting these goals that we must be constantly aware of new avenues to pursue. Here are a few examples using the *Mathematics Exploration Toolkit* (MET).

What is the largest number that can be written with three digits? Typically, students ask if the same digit may be used over again, and then offer 999, 99^9, or 9^{99} as solutions. Eventually, through prompting or after some thought, 99^9 enters the discussion. A symbolic manipulator gives exact values for 999, 99^9, and 9^{99}, so 999 goes quickly out of contention (see **Figure 1**).

One avenue of discussion concerns which of 99^9 and 9^{99} is larger. There are several different ways to deal with this question. Rounding and approximation can be used in saying that 9 is close to 10 and 99 is close to 100. Then 99^9 is approximately 100^{10} and 9^{99} is approximately 10^{100}. Now $100^{10} = (10^2)^{10} = 10^{20}$ is equivalent to 1 followed by 20 zeros, while 10^{100} is equivalent to 1 followed by 100 zeros. Thus, 10^{100} is larger, and so 9^{99} is greater than 99^9.

Using laws of exponents, $9^{99} = (9^9)(9^{11})(9^{79})$ and $99^9 = (9^9)(11^9)$. Both expressions can be divided by 9^9, leaving $(9^{11})(9^{79})$ and 11^9. However, for $x > 2$, $x^{(x+2)} > (x + 2)^x$, so $9^{11} > 11^9$, and 9^{79} has not been considered yet. Again, 9^{99} is greater than 99^9.

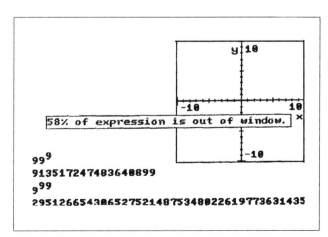

99^9
913517247483648899
9^{99}
295126654306527521487534802261977363 1435

FIGURE 1. A SYMBOLIC MANIPULATOR GIVES EXACT VALUES FOR 99^9 AND 9^{99}.

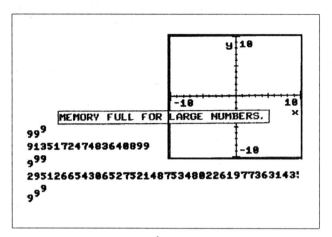

FIGURE 2. EVIDENCE THAT 99^{9^9} IS GREATEST.

Dealing with 99^{9^9} inserts a new set of difficulties. First, few symbolic manipulators are capable of handling such a huge number. (See **Figure 2**.) It has over 365,000,000 digits! If it were typed using ten digits per inch, the result would be over 550 miles long! A word processor would use 1800 sheets of paper to print an equivalent message (assuming no spaces between periods).

The problem provides an excellent opportunity to demonstrate thinking patterns often used by mathematicians. When a problem involves large numbers, investigate another problem with smaller values. Use a similar setting and look for patterns.

Work with 2's and look at 22^2, 2^{22}, and 2^{2^2}. Determine which of the three is largest by using a computer or calculator (**Figure 3**).

$$22^2 = 484$$
$$2^{22} = 4,194,304$$
$$2^{2^2} = 16$$

This does not fit the pattern suggested by the 9's.

Look at another example using 3's (**Figure 4**).

$$33^3 = 35,937$$
$$3^{33} = 5,559,060,566,555,523$$
$$3^{3^3} = 7,625,597,484,987$$

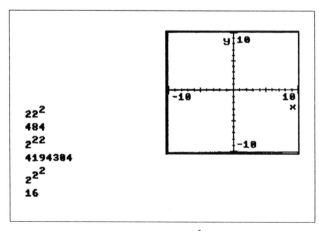

FIGURE 3. WHICH OF 22^2, 2^{22}, AND 2^{2^2} IS LARGEST?

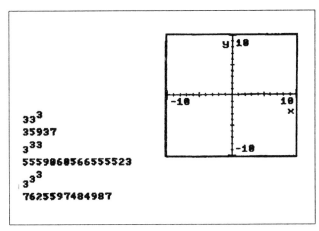

FIGURE 4. WHICH OF 33^3, 3^{33}, AND 33^{3^3} IS LARGEST?

This does not seem to fit the pattern where the power to the power has the largest value, but it does appear to be getting closer to what is expected. Investigation of the second and third entries in each set shows a much larger relative change between the third elements and encourages a look at the same setup with 4's. Students are often told not to base a judgment on two examples only; that idea is illustrated here and in **Figure 5**.

$$44^4 = 3,748,096$$
$$4^{44} = 309,485,009,821,345,068,724,781,056$$
$$4^{4^4} = \text{a number with 155 digits!}$$

Now it can be seen that the power to the power will yield the largest value.

This example provides a wonderful opportunity for exponential growth discussion as well as the impact of exponent size. In addition, laws of exponents can be used to approach which of the three situations within any set should be the largest and why.

Two other discussions can be approached from this situation. Students in this lesson should be familiar with the order of operations: **P**arentheses, **E**xponents, **M**ultiply, **D**ivide, **A**dd, **S**ubtract (PEMDAS). However, what is the rule for the third element of the set, A^{B^C}? Is that $\left(A^B\right)^C$ or is it $A^{\left(B^C\right)}$? In other words, is the problem worked from the top down or from the bottom up?

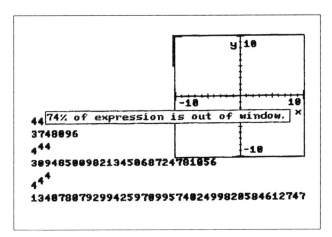

FIGURE 5. USING 4'S AS ANOTHER EXAMPLE.

Many advanced students are not aware of the answer to this question. Substitute 2, 3, and 4 for *A*, *B*, and *C*, respectively, and use appropriate software to resolve the issue quickly (**Figure 6**).

Finally, if you are fortunate enough to have software that does not wrap or scroll when expanding 4^{4^4}, a very nice patterning example is available. What is the last digit in 4^{4^4}? Typically, 1, 3, 5, 7, and 9 are quickly eliminated because the base is even, and so all its counting-number powers must be even. Generally, 0 can be taken out of the discussion because at least one factor of 5 would be needed with one of the factors of 4 to get a 0, but in this situation, the *only* factors are 4. That still leaves 2, 4, 6, or 8 with no apparent route of investigation to follow.

Switching tactics and realizing that

$$4^1 = 4$$
$$4^2 = 16$$
$$4^3 = 64$$
$$4^4 = 256,$$

a pattern is provided in the last digit of each response, and the idea given that 4^{4^4} must end either in 4 or in 6. Since the odd powers end in 4 and the even powers end in 6, the only thing left to determine is whether this is an odd or even power. Once that is done, the response that 4^{4^4} ends in a 6 comes rather quickly.

This lesson could be taught without technology by supplying evaluations. However, the impact of the lesson is severely restricted if the situations are not worked out in real time with the students. ❑

$$A^{B^C}$$
$$2^{3^4}$$
$$2^{3^4} = 2417851639229258349412352$$
$$(2^3)^4 = 8^4$$
$$4096 = 4096$$
$$2^{3^4} = 2^{81}$$
$$2417851639229258349412352 = 2417851639229$$

FIGURE 6. SUBSTITUTE 2, 3, AND 4 FOR *A*, *B*, AND *C*.

The National Council of Teachers of Mathematics (NCTM) emphasized in its *Curriculum and Evaluation Standards for School Mathematics* that "new technology not only has made calculations and graphing easier, it has changed the very nature of the problems important to mathematics and the methods mathematicians use to investigate them." Doug Brumbaugh ably demonstrates how average students may explore with a computer algebra system significant mathematics that would otherwise remain beyond their reach. This gives students the power to investigate a problem as a working mathematician would approach it.

There are several computer algebra systems (also called *symbolic manipulators*) available on desktop computers, including *Derive* and *Mathematics Exploration Toolkit* (MET) for MS-DOS machines, and *Algebra Xpresser* and *Theorist* for the Macintosh. *Mathcad, Maple*, and *Mathematica* all run on both PCs (DOS or Windows) and Macs.

In addition to the fine examples that Doug Brumbaugh provides, teachers may also use a computer algebra system in the search for prime numbers. Throughout history, mathematicians have sought a simple formula that would generate prime numbers. The seventeenth century mathematician Pierre de Fermat suggested that any number of the form $2^{(2^n)} + 1$ would be prime. In his honor, such numbers are called *Fermat numbers*.

The first six Fermat numbers are shown in a *Mathcad* document, **Figure 7**. To determine whether each is a prime, we must try to factor it. That onerous task is best left to a computer algebra system, and *Mathcad* makes quick work of it.

Fermat determined that the first five of these numbers are indeed prime. He died in 1665 still believing that his formula generated prime numbers. Not until a century later, in 1732, was Leonhard Euler able to establish that the sixth Fermat number is composite. Today, it takes a student's desktop computer only a few seconds to resolve this. Mathematicians now wonder whether there is even one other prime Fermat number besides those Fermat himself knew.

With a computer algebra system to do the tedious computations, students may investigate other potential prime number generators, such as $4n + 3$, $6n + 5$, $n^2 - n + 41$, and $n^2 - 79n + 1601$. ❏

Fermat Numbers: n = 0, 1, 2, 3, 4, 5

$2^{(2^0)} + 1$ expands to   3

$2^{(2^1)} + 1$ expands to   5

$2^{(2^2)} + 1$ expands to   17

$2^{(2^3)} + 1$ expands to   257

$2^{(2^4)} + 1$ expands to   65537

$2^{(2^5)} + 1$ expands to   4294967297

           by factoring, yields   (641)·(6700417)

FIGURE 7. THE FIRST SIX FERMAT NUMBERS.